"I WAS PAID TO BE A WARHEAD —AND ANYONE WHO CAME NEAR ME SHOULD GET KNOCKED INTO HELL!"

Jack Tatum

"If professional football is really about some of the things he says it is, then maybe those of us who really enjoy the game had better ask ourselves who we are and what we are about."

Jerry Izenberg, *New York Post*

"It's frightening, it casts doubt on a whole way of life, and it indicts a national institution . . . a casebook study on the destruction of a young athlete by a cruel system."

Jim Murray, *Los Angeles Times*

"It will make you wince . . . It may well be the most interesting sports book ever written."

Bob Padecky, *Sacramento Bee*

"Courageously frank . . . uncommonly sharp . . . The shock and anger people feel over Tatum's book has been running wild . . . Everybody grab the sides of the chair and hold on."

Mike Antonucci, *San Jose Mercury*

THEY CALL ME ASSASSIN

JACK TATUM
with Bill Kushner

 AVON
PUBLISHERS OF BARD, CAMELOT AND DISCUS BOOKS

AVON BOOKS
A division of
The Hearst Corporation
959 Eighth Avenue
New York, New York 10019

Copyright © 1979 by John David Tatum and W. Joseph Kushner
Published by arrangement with Everest House
Library of Congress Catalog Card Number: 79-51202
ISBN: 0-380-52480-5

First Avon Printing, October, 1980
Second Printing

AVON TRADEMARK REG. U.S. PAT. OFF. AND IN
OTHER COUNTRIES, MARCA REGISTRADA,
HECHO EN U.S.A.

Printed in the U.S.A.

CONTENTS

I PLEAD GUILTY, BUT ONLY TO AGGRESSIVE PLAY

When you're a two-time All-American from Ohio State, you expect to be drafted into professional football. I certainly felt that one of the NFL teams would draft me, and in the first round, too. In college, and even in high school, I had developed a reputation as a devastating hitter. Whenever I'd hit a running back or receiver with a good shot, the man usually didn't get up. I've always had an affinity for controlled violence and contact sports. Professional scouts look for athletes who have an appetite for contact, so they were looking at me.

Before the draft, the All-American team did a television show with Mr. Bob Hope. He introduced the team members and cracked jokes about each player. When my turn came, he said, "Jack Tatum . . . what a hitter. Tatum can straighten your spine quicker than Ben Casey. Why, he's so tough that even his fingernails have muscles. I became a Jack Tatum fan when I saw him play in the Rose Bowl. Jack hit O. J. [Simpson] so hard that he knocked me out of my fifty yard line seat and into the parking lot. Imagine how the Juice felt . . . squeezed. Jack's mother told me that he was just a normal kid . . . except he liked to ram his head into fire hydrants. Normal kid, eh?"

Mr. Hope glanced at me and saw that I was laughing and enjoying his teasing. He paused for a second and then said, "Sorry we don't have any fire hydrants on stage, Jack. Oh, what the hell, if you want to have some of your kind of fun, then go ahead and ram your head into the walls."

Neither Mr. Hope nor anyone in the audience realized what was really making me laugh, but the conception most people have of aggressive football players seem so funny to me. They think a man has to be mentally unbalanced to play football violently. I know me better than anyone else knows me, and I'm no psychopath. But I and others like myself learned early in our careers that in football, the name of the game is hitting, and to play it well, you have to play it hard.

High school football was the beginning of my career. I quickly learned that it hurt more to get hit than it did to actually do the hitting. That might sound strange, but let me explain. Most high school defensive players are passive. They sit back and wait for the opposition to come to them. This is bad, because a young player can get seriously hurt. When you lay back, the offensive man builds up his momentum and is doing the hitting while the defensive man is getting hit.

Good defensive football amounts to mass times velocity. The faster I can move toward impact, and the more violently I can drive my body through a target, the more effective my hit will be. This way I'm doing the hitting and the offensive player is absorbing the punishment. Most running backs and receivers never run full speed. They're either cutting or dodging tacklers. So once I figure out where the man is trying to go, it just becomes a matter of building up a full head of speed and driving through him. My method is similar to a karate punch. I concentrate on a point one yard or so beyond the man I'm going after, and on impact, I drive hard to that point.

I played my first game of football as a sophomore in high school, and even then I was effective. My coach, John Federici, said, "Jack, when you see the quarterback dropping back to pass, go after him."

I did something right because in the fourth quarter, the team we were playing ran out of quarterbacks. They had to finish the game with a tight end taking snaps from the center. After the game, I was a hero. The fans loved my style of play.

In college I developed quickly. I grew stronger and faster, and became a more aggressive and vicious tackler. Naturally, I still practiced the basics of sound football, but in addition, I also learned other important defensive fundamentals. Coach Woody Hayes was a teacher of body control. He believed that a great athlete could thoroughly control his body. Through Woody's drills I learned how to start and stop on a dime and generate maximum power in my tackles. An important part of body control was also, as Woody called it, mind control. This meant no late hits or cheap shots out of bounds. It was still rough and violent football, but my style of aggressive play was within the rules and regulations of the game.

In my first collegiate game I won no All-American honors, but I did make the other teams on our schedule wary of me. I was only a sophomore, but I had earned a starting assignment as a linebacker. We were playing Southern Methodist, a school known for putting the ball in the air. That meant people would be running pass patterns in my area looking for the ball instead of the linebackers. Believe me, when you catch someone with a good shot who isn't expecting it, you're going to hurt him.

Early in the first quarter I spotted a wide receiver running a quick slant over the middle. The receiver was concentrating on making the catch and never saw me coming. He was my first collegiate knockout victim.

Later in the same period, I saw a running back slip over the middle and look back for the pass. He became my second knockout. The 85,000 fans watching the game were delighted. The action was gruesome, but that's what the fans love, violent contact. The Ohio State fans loved the action I had provided and so did my coaches. Once again I was a hero.

By the time my college career ended, I had more knockouts than Joe Louis and Muhammad Ali combined. I won every defensive award the Big Ten had to offer and more. Three times I was among the top vote getters for the Heisman Trophy, and twice I was voted the nation's best defensive player. I was certain that my next adventure would be professional football.

I have mentioned a word that is synonymous with boxing: Knockout. Actually, though, knockouts do occur in many of the nonpassive sports. It's just that the very purpose of a boxing match is built around one's ability to knock his opponent into a senseless mass of blood and flesh. Football and the other contact sports do have a different purpose. In football there are various degrees of violence and contact, but the two basic objectives of the game are to score points and prevent points from being scored, and not to knock people out cold. However, when you put an offensive team on the field for the purpose of advancing the ball forward, and the defensive team has quite the opposite purpose, it all becomes a war, and I am simply a warrior in a very physical way. As a warrior I must discourage running backs and receivers whenever they attempt to gain yardage against the defense. It is a physical and a violent job, and quite often the end results are knockouts or serious injuries to my opponent. But it is just part of a very risky business.

The first round of the college draft went as I expected, and I became the property of the Oakland Raiders. After eight years of hard work in high school and college, I was at last part of the NFL.

Several weeks after the draft, I flew out to Oakland for contract talks with Al Davis, a partner and general manager of the Raiders. Al Davis talked my language. I asked, "How much?" and he answered with a $50,000 bonus check and a three-year, no-cut contract worth six attractive figures. I signed the contract.

When the paperwork was finished, there was a statement in the press to the effect the Raiders had just hired the Assassin that no winning team could be without . . . and his name was Jack Tatum.

"Assassin?" I thought. "That makes me sound like a gangster." But, actually, I was a "hit man." I didn't rush out and buy a dark suit or fedora, but I did think about my career. The Raiders had invested in me and I had to produce. Professional football is vicious and brutal; there's not much time for sentiment. I was being paid well for a service, and if I didn't deliver, they'd go and find someone else who would.

I was committed to play my first professional game with the College All-Stars against the World Champion Baltimore Colts. The game was an annual charity affair held each year in Chicago, but it was also much more.

As All-Americans we wanted to prove to the Colts that we belonged in the NFL. We weren't concerned with showing off or pretending that we were already professional superstars. We just wanted to go out, play a good game, and earn the respect of the best team in professional football. But for some reason the old pros turned nasty and tried to beat our heads in. Every time they got off a good play, they would smart-mouth us or cuss. I thought it was very unfair of them to treat us as if we didn't belong in the same stadium. We had only played together for ten days, and the Colts had years behind them. I don't think that any of the All-Stars seriously believed that we could win the game, but still, we didn't expect to be disgraced.

Before very long, the Colts had a seven-point lead but were acting as though they had a seventy-point lead. On a third down and eight play, I started thinking that maybe Earl Morrall would look for his tight end, John Mackey. Earlier in the game Morrall tried a quick pass to the tight end, and it had worked for good yardage. That first time, as I went after Mackey, someone had partially blocked me and I hadn't made good contact. Mackey got up, shrugged his shoulders, and walked back to the huddle laughing and hollering in my direction, "Hard-hitting rookie . . . what a joke."

Morrall took the snap and dropped straight back looking for the tight end. I carefully avoided the blind side blocks and drew a bead on Mackey's rib cage. Morrall hadn't thrown one of his better passes, and I could have easily intercepted, but I had other plans. I wondered if John Mackey would still think I was a joke after he was really hit. As Mackey reached back for the ball, I drove my helmet into his ribs and knocked him to the ground. It was a good hit. Mackey was on the ground flopping around like a wounded duck and gasping for air. Standing over him, I glared down and asked,

"How funny was that joke?" Of course, I admit I cussed at him, too.

John Mackey wasn't the only Colt I ran into on that particular night. Later in the game I found another tight end, Tom Mitchell, roaming in my area trying to catch one of Morrall's terrible wobbly passes. I introduced myself to Tom, but I don't think he heard the name. Tom was my second professional knockout.

Immediately, sportswriters started comparing me with Dick Butkus, a linebacker for the Chicago Bears. Butkus was supposedly the meanest, dirtiest, hardest-hitting football player to ever put on a pair of cleats and walk out onto the field. I resented the comparison because I had seen Butkus play. I admit that Butkus was mean and there was strong evidence he played dirty (teeth marks on running backs' ankles), but for anyone to think he was a hitter was absurd. Butkus even admitted that he couldn't hit. When he traveled across the country doing TV shows, he said, "Whenever I get a clear shot at the ball carrier, I don't want him turning around to see who did the hitting. I want him to know without looking that it was Dick Butkus."

Any fool knows that when you hit someone with your best shot and he is still able to think, then you're not a hitter. My idea of a good hit is when the victim wakes up on the sidelines with train whistles blowing in his head and wondering who he is and what ran over him. I'm not saying that Butkus wasn't a fair linebacker, because after all, he was an All-Pro. But in my estimation Butkus was most definitely not a hitter.

As a defensive player I had resigned myself to the fact that I would never rush for 1,000 yards during a season and I would never score many touchdowns. But at the same time I vowed to earn my reputation in professional football with aggressive tackling. I knew that in professional football or even high school football, the team that can dominate physically will usually win. Punishment is demoralizing, and few teams can withstand a painful beating without it warping their will to win. I never make a tackle just to bring someone down. I want to punish the man I'm going after and I want him to know that it's going to hurt every time he comes my way.

Violent play can make a defensive team much sharper, but there is a limit. I believe that running backs and receivers are fair game once they step onto the field. If they want to run out of bounds to avoid the tackle, then fine, let them run away from the action. But anyone that comes near me is going to get hit. I like to believe that my best hits border on felonious assault, but at the same time everything I do is by the rule book. I don't want to be the heir to Butkus's title, because his career had shadows. Some people say that Butkus bit, while others say he didn't. My style of play is mean and nasty and I am going to beat people physically and mentally, but in no way am I going down in the record book as a cheap-shot artist.

After the All-Star game I joined the Raider training camp at Santa Rosa, California. I guess it was surprising that my helmet still fit over my head. I was starting to believe everything the press wrote about me, and I'm afraid I became overconfident. After all, I was considered a superstar in high school and I was a collegiate All-American two times. Then came the All-Star game and my two professional knockouts. It was a lot for a twenty-one-year-old man to grasp and still keep both feet on the ground. The Oakland Raiders had a man named Fred Biletnikoff, now retired, who put things in proper perspective for me, however.

Fred Biletnikoff was a balding but hippy-looking wide receiver for the Oakland Raiders. When I was instructed by my coaches to cover Fred one-on-one during a pass defense drill, I laughed to myself. Fred Biletnikoff had a great pair of hands and could catch anything near him, but he was slow by NFL standards. I've played aganist big receivers, small receivers, and fast receivers, and they couldn't burn me. Now, for my first test in an Oakland Raider camp, they put me against a slow receiver.

Fred ran his first pattern and I showed him why I was all All-American. Covering him like a blanket, I nearly intercepted the ball, and after the play I told Fred, "You're lucky that we aren't hitting."

On the next play Fred drove off the line hard and made a good move to the outside. I was too quick for him though and reacted like an All-Pro. But then he broke back across the middle and left me tripping over my own feet. Needless to say, the quarterback laid a perfect pass into Fred's hands, and he scored. On the way back to the huddle, Fred showed me the football and asked, "Were you looking for this, Rookie?"

That got me upset and I started cussing. I told him, "Try me again and see what happens, Chump!"

Fred came at me again with about five different fakes and just as I went left, he went right and scored again. Fred Biletnikoff started running patterns that quickly deflated my ego and taught me humiliation. He burned me time and time again so bad that I went back to the locker room feeling very uncertain as to whether or not I had what it takes to make it in professional football. Deep down inside my pride was scorched.

Later that same evening I bumped into Fred and we started talking about practice. Fred turned out to be a pretty good guy. After a few minutes we were talking like old friends. Fred told me that he grew up in Erie, Pennsylvania, and it didn't sound like paradise. While he was talking about the mills and factories of Erie, I was picturing the filth and dirt of my hometown, Passaic, New Jersey. After a great high school career in Erie, Fred accepted a scholarship to attend Florida State University, and there earned All-American honors. The more we talked, the better I liked the man.

"A man has to adjust," Fred was saying about the NFL, "and if he doesn't, he's gone. The difference today was that I knew you could knock me out if you hit me with a good shot but you didn't know that I could burn you. Now it comes down to respecting each other and adjusting."

I listened to everything Fred told me, because he had the experience and wanted to help my career. He told me that receivers are the biggest bunch of cons going. Fred warned, "Some receivers will fake with their hips, feet, head, shoulders, eyes, or anything to gain a liberated step. Don't be sucked in by a fake; go after what's real. Remember, Jack, all the quarterbacks in this league can hit the one-on-one pass. If some receiver gives you a fake and you trip over your own feet going after nothing, then it's just God and green grass between that man and six points."

Fred started working with me and taught me how to think like a receiver. By the time the exhibition season opened up, I didn't have all the answers, but I gave my best. Maybe if Fred hadn't given me some of his time, my stay in the NFL would have been a short one.

I got burned a few times, but luck was with me. It seemed that if a receiver caught a pass over me, I was able to stick the next attempt in his rib cage. Still, though, I was undisciplined enough to be hazardous. Aggressiveness is as common to football as helmets and shoulder pads, but I had yet to learn how to channel my aggressive style of play into aspects of the game where it would do the team the most good.

In one game we were holding a 21–14 lead over the New Orleans Saints. Late in the fourth period the Saints quarterback threw over the middle for his wide receiver, Danny Abramowicz, who was well covered by our strong safety, George Atkinson. In my eagerness to assist, I blasted in from the weak side and creamed everyone. It was a double knockout. I got Abramowicz, but I got George too.

After that my play became sloppy. I'd go after the ball and slam into anyone that got in the way. It was early in the season and I had already knocked out seven men. That would have been a good start, except that four of those knockouts were Oakland Raiders. I knocked out our Captain, Willie Brown, got Nemiah Wilson and cut his eye pretty bad, too, and then there was George Atkinson. I knocked out George twice. It got to the point where our defensive people were starting to worry more about me than the real enemy.

After George recovered from his second knockout, he took me aside and said, "Damn, Tate, are you color-blind or something? I wear the same color jersey as you do. I'm on your side and the deal is gettin' the other team."

After he felt that I was sure which team I played for, George started teaching me some of his techniques. I learned how to anticipate the offensive man. For example, if a running back went wide on a play and there was good outside pursuit, then I'd position myself inside and hope the back would cut against the flow. That way I'd be waiting, and from there it was a matter of building up my speed and hitting the enemy. On passing situations I talked with the other defensive backs and asked how they were going to play a particular receiver. That way I sort of knew where my people were going to be and how they were going to play the situation. For example, if Willie Brown said he was going to play his man loose and go for the ball, then I went for the receiver. It started working so well that most of the time I let the other backs go for the interception and I'd punish the receiver.

George Atkinson started teaching me a few more of his other tricks. George said, "I was going to teach you the 'Hook' when you first came into the league but you were having identification problems. Now that you seem to know who's who, let me show you the best intimidator in the business, the Hook." Of course, the rules governing the Hook have changed recently, but back then it wasn't just legal but an important weapon in a good hitter's arsenal.

The Hook is simply flexing your biceps and trying to catch the receiver's head in the joint between the forearm and upper arm. It's like hitting with the biceps by using a headlock type of action. The purpose of the Hook was to strip the receiver of the ball, his helmet, his head, and his courage. Of course, you only use the Hook in full-speed contact, and usually from the blind side. Using the Hook effectively was not as easy as it may sound. Very few defensive backs used the Hook because if you were a little high with your shot, the receiver would slip under and get away. Also, if you weren't careful and you hit with the forearm, it became an illegal tactic.

Another trick that George taught me was the "Groundhog." The Groundhog is a perfectly timed hit to the ankles just as the receiver is leaping high to catch a pass. The Groundhog isn't as devastating as it looks on TV but it does have a tendency to keep the receiver closer to the ground on high passes.

As the free safety for the Raiders, I never have a specific responsibility. I am given the freedom to help out wherever we feel the offense is going to concentrate its attack. If a team is running good against us, then I move closer to the line of scrimmage and try to get a good hit on a running back. Most of the time one good hit will slow down any running back and wake up the defense. That's what I meant about punishment demoralizing and warping a team's will to win.

I started feeling comfortable about halfway into the season. It seemed as though everything was falling into place rather nicely, and best of all, I hadn't knocked out any of my teammates for three games. I worked hard at practice, studied game films of coming opponents, and showed improvement weekly. My career was getting off to a solid start, and I felt good about the overall development I had shown. I was doing my job, getting well-paid, and no one had any complaints. At least no one on the Oakland Raiders had any complaints.

If ever a man did have a reason to complain about my style of play, it had to be Riley Odoms, a tight end with the Denver Broncos. During a game at Denver's Mile High Stadium, I leveled the best shot of my career against Riley. It was a clean hit, not a cheap shot, but I was upset because I really thought I had killed the man.

Late in the game we had built a 27–16 lead, but Denver's offense was getting fancy. They singled out Nemiah Wilson, our left cornerback, as the man in the secondary to exploit. Nemo was small, only about 170 pounds, and he was playing with an injured leg. This seemed to be an invitation for Charley Johnson, Denver's quarterback, to do his passing around Nemo. Denver positioned both of their wide receivers on opposite sides of the field, away from Nemo, and put him one-on-one with Riley Odoms. Riley is one of the best tight ends in professional football. He's big, standing 6 feet 4 inches and weighing 235 pounds; he would be a lot of man for Nemo on this particular Sunday, or any day of the week, for that matter.

Since I had the option of roaming around and policing the secondary, I decided to help Nemo. When the play started to develop, I dropped back a few steps to give Riley the impression I had deep coverage. Riley saw me dropping off and made a quick move over the middle. It was a great move because Riley had Nemo off balance and he broke open by five yards. Quarterbacks love to see that type of a situation, and Charley Johnson wasted little time releasing the ball toward Riley. I just timed my hit. When I felt I could zero in on Riley's head at the same time the ball arrived in his hands, I moved. It was a perfectly timed hit, and I used my Hook on his head. Because of the momentum built up by the angles and speed of both Riley and myself, it was the best hit of my career. I heard Riley scream on impact and felt his body go limp. He landed flat on his back, and the ball came to rest on his chest for a completion, but Riley's eyes rolled back in his head and he wasn't breathing. I had another knockout, and maybe this time, I had even killed a man. God knew that I didn't want something like that to happen.

I've used the word "kill," and when I'm hitting someone I really am trying to kill, but not like forever. I mean I'm trying to kill the play or the pass, but not the man. Football is a violent game, and people are seriously injured; sometimes they are killed. But any man that puts on a uniform and doesn't play hard is cheating. The players of the NFL are paid good money and risk serious injuries because the structure of football is based on punishing your opponent. There is nothing humorous or even vaguely cheerful about playing in the NFL. It is a high risk but high-salaried job.

Riley was scraped off the field and carried to the sidelines. He was shaken and hurt, but thank God he was still alive. After the game I went over to the Denver locker room and talked with Riley. He said, "Damn, Tate, don't ever hit me like that again. You nearly killed me." Then he laughed and I slapped him on the back and smiled with relief. Very few people understand the camaraderie and mutual respect professional athletes feel for each other. We admire each other's abilities and appreciate the man who has the guts to do his job well. My coaches, sportswriters, and even football fans talked about how hard I hit Riley. People called that hit everything from vicious to brutal but I never heard anyone say it was a cheap shot.

During the years that have followed I have continued my style of play and have registered many more knockouts. I remember one game, again it was against Denver, when the Broncos' best running back, Floyd Little, took a hand off and swept around left end with a herd of blockers leading the way. As he turned the corner, the reds and blues of Denver had gone south and I was coming up fast. Floyd didn't see me coming and there was a collision at mid-field near the sidelines, right in front of the Denver bench. I whipped my Hook up under Floyd's face mask and landed a solid shot flush on his jaw. Floyd looked like a magician practicing levitation just before all the lights went out. His head snapped back, his feet straightened out, and the ball and one of his shoes shot into the stands. I was coming so hard that my momentum carried both of us into the Denver bench.

The play had started close to the sidelines and I could have pushed Floyd out of bounds, but instead, I hit him with everything I had to offer because if you just push a guy like Floyd Little out of bounds, then he'll start getting some bad ideas about you. Floyd would probably start thinking that I was soft, and that would lead to him wanting to take advantage of me. Before long every team in the NFL would be gunning their game plans at me, and when that happened the Raiders would get someone else, someone that would beat a running back out of bounds rather than give him a sissy push.

Some of the players moaned when I hit Floyd and a few of them even cussed at me, but once again no one even suggested that I hit Floyd with a cheap shot.

My ferocity seemed to influence the entire Raider defense. Everyone started talking about getting a "knockout." Guys who used to tackle just to bring someone down started to punish people, and that made the defense much sharper. If a running back got off a good play and picked up, say, fifteen yards but got his head rattled so badly that he had to leave the game, it was worth the fifteen yards. I started taking shots at everyone wearing a different colored uniform. I'd take shots at every receiver and running back. They didn't like it, and sometimes they'd send a lineman after me, but I didn't care; I'd take a shot at him, too. I would initiate a demoralizing kind of punishment on the opposing offense and it picked our defensive team up. The Raiders had become a nasty group of men. The Oakland Raiders have never tried to look loveable. As soon as they run onto the field, they radiate villainy. The black-shirted Raiders, with their crossed swords and pirate decals, immediately bring to mind the bad guys in the old movies. Every team in professional football seems to consider the Raiders their arch-rival. They all treat the Raider malice with a special intensity, and football fans love it. I was enjoying my job with the Raiders and proud to be a part of the organization regardless of what the national image was. I knew in my heart that it was professional football and there wasn't any on-field charm connected with the game.

During my second year George Atkinson suggested that he and I start a contest for who would get the most knockouts over the course of the season. It sounded like a good idea, and we agreed on a set of rules. First of all, neither of us wanted to get penalties called against us so we agreed that our hits must be clean shots and legal. Next, the man you hit would have to be down for an official injury time-out and he had to be helped off the field. That would be considered a "knockout" and it was worth two points. Sometimes, one of us would hit a man and he'd take the injury time-out but would limp off the field under his own power. We called that a "limp-off" and it was worth one point. When the season started, so did we. Actually, it was all part of our job, but we made a game out of it. Guess who won?

The seasons had a way of piling up, and before I knew it, I was a veteran of seven years. When I stopped to look back and see what had happened over the course of my career, I was shocked. I came into the NFL wanting to be the most intimidating hitter in the history of the game. At this stage of my career, people were scared of me because they knew I was accomplishing my objective. But something else was also happening and I resented it. Some people considered me a dirty player and a cheap-shot artist. I can live with rumors, but when I see my name published in the San Diego *Union* along with football's top ten dirty players, I get upset. When my attorney calls me from Pittsburgh and tells me that Sam Nover of Channel 2 and Myron Cope of Channel 4 are doing specials on my dirty tactics, I become angry. After a few questionable incidents, everything has mushroomed into a problem serious enough for Howard Cosell to dedicate one of his half-time shows on "Monday Night Football" to George Atkinson and me and our "cheap shots." Even NBC Sports used prime time for a special, "Violence in Sports."

It started with a normal football game, a few good hits, a knockout, and a certain coach's "criminal element" speech. From there it was picked up by the press and traveled into the office of the Commissioner of the NFL. From there some fines were issued, which then I refused to pay, and now every official in the NFL is throwing quick flags in my general direction. However, I doubt that I'm going to change how I live my life or how I play the game because, as I told the Commissioner, "I plead guilty, but only to aggressive play."

THE
CRIMINAL ELEMENTS

In all sports there are bitterly contested rivalries. Ali and Frazier fought three times with a ferocious intensity that would have had lesser men crying for mercy. Connors and Borg swatted tennis balls as though they were beating each other's heads in with racquets. And each year, late in November, Ohio State and Michigan duel in a death struggle that usually determines the Big Ten Championship. But when the game is over, a great athlete realizes the battle is also over and walks away with a genuine feeling of respect for his opponent.

During my career, I have often risen to the heights of a tremendous effort when it came time to battle the rival gang, the rival high school football team, or whatever. As I grew in physical size and developed techniques and mental abilities, my competition also seemed to grow, the rivalry became a much more serious situation. In college the rival was Michigan; I was a winner twice and a loser once. However, in college victory or defeat was only a matter of pride, whereas in professional football it is quite another story.

In professional football every team becomes another team's natural enemy whenever they play against each other. Still, there are special rivalries that seem to bring a higher degree of intensity to the contest. Personally, I play every game hard and violently, but when I go against the Pittsburgh Steelers a different style of aggression seems to come over me. In fact, an intensely aggressive mood sweeps through the entire Raider team.

The same feeling overcomes the Pittsburgh players as they ready themselves to go against us. When this type of situation develops, you have a very special game. Both Pittsburgh and Oakland consider themselves the best in professional football, and when we meet we spend a violent Sunday afternoon trying to convince the other team of that point. Those are the games that become more than just a matter of pride or winning and losing. The professional success, security, and esteem of every individual on both the Steelers and the Raiders depends on his performance in "the big one." Any player can be having the best season of his career, but if he muffs it in this game, everyone—the fans, his teammates, and the owners—will quickly forget all his previous accomplishments and remember only that this was the season when he threw the interception, or fumbled, or missed a tackle in the Oakland-Pittsburgh game. Yes, we call it a game, but it just happens to be our livelihood and a segment of our future existence. With stakes so high, the game becomes a serious situation. I, for one, would rather get burned ten times against the New York Giants than once against the Steelers.

September 5, 1976, wasn't a typical Sunday in my life. I started the day off in a normal fashion with a shower and a light breakfast, but I was moody and much quieter than usual. I was still trying to shake some of the cobwebs from those conscious chambers of my mind and get serious. The previous night we had had a party with some of my teammates and a few of the Pittsburgh Steelers. It wasn't a wild drinking party, just sort of a get-together with a few ladies, a few laughs, and a glass or two of a mild wine. Even then I could feel the tension building, and that wasn't normal. Usually, whenever we get together with the Steelers for a game, Saturday night and Sunday afternoon become two separate segments of life. We share the mutual friendship and respect of athletes on Saturday night with the understanding that we will be temporary enemies on Sunday. But somehow this particular Saturday night seemed to have a little Sunday flavor in it. It wasn't a good party, because everyone was tense. We joked and laughed a little, but most of it was phony. Everyone could sense it, and we all knew right there, Sunday afternoon was going to be hell.

I want to be alone before the game. I don't want to talk with reporters or teammates, I just want to be alone. I spend that time in my own way mentally getting ready for the game. Sports fans can never realize the pressure on a professional athlete. I work and train a lifetime for two or three hours that put my talents against the best receivers and running backs in the world. I know they will try to burn me, and my job is to discourage them. It is a war in every sense of the word, and I am a warrior. Those hours before the game are lonely and tough. I think about, and even fear, what can happen. I know that in a split second of contact someone could get seriously injured or even killed, but at the same time I realize it is my job and the way of my life I have chosen. To back down or even think about backing down would be cheating. So when the ball is set for play, I am ready to use whatever means of my physical or mental ability it will take to protect myself and be effective in my job.

While driving to the stadium I started thinking about our game with the Steelers last season. Late in December we had played in Pittsburgh for the championship of the American Football Conference. Pittsburgh won the game and went on to win the Super Bowl. That really dug at me, even though I had played a great game. I wanted to win. I wanted the Super Bowl and the extra money, but Pittsburgh was there. I stayed home and sullenly watched the game on television.

Then I started thinking about Lynn Swann. Last year, on the ice of Three Rivers Stadium, I caught Lynn Swann running a pattern across the middle. I hit him! I hit him hard and he went down. Then several plays later George hit him. In fact, Lynn spent a week in the hospital with a serious concussion, but still he recovered in time to win the MVP award at the Super Bowl.

My collision with Lynn Swann was, I admit, premeditated. I saw him coming across the middle for a pass, and even though Terry Bradshaw had thrown the ball in a different direction, Swann was still a fair and legal target. I don't want Lynn Swann or anyone in my area trying to catch passes. Most receivers know I earn my money and reputation with devasting hits. I don't care, but when the receiver operates as the primary target, I'm going to make him pay the price. A receiver needs concentration to succeed. If by using demoralizing hits I can get the receiver to start thinking about me instead of catching the ball, I will win the battle.

Against the Steelers last season I was only doing a job, but before the game was over I had been hit in the knees with a cheap shot because of the Swann action. Ray Mansfield, the Steelers' center, saw me cream Swann and, in what he thought to be an act of big-brother justice, hit me with a spearing cheap shot. Several plays after Swann had been carried off the field, George Atkinson and I smashed into Rocky Bleier and he fumbled. Bodies were all over the ground scrambling for the ball, but instead of Mansfield thinking about recovering the fumble, he speared me in the knee. Some of the teams in the NFL try to intimidate defensive backs by sending linemen at them, but I don't think it was a Steeler plan as much as a Mansfield idea. Still, the end result was an injury to my knee.

There is a difference between my hit on Swann and Mansfield's hit on me. Swann was a legal target, and so was I. What I mean is that on that particular play Lynn Swann could have blocked me. On the other hand, I had the right to take him out of the play. I admit it was full speed, and I did hit him high with a Hook, but still, it was legal. There was an official on the play, but no flag. Mansfield, on the other hand, admits he tried to "get me" because I got Swann. Ray Mansfield succeeded, but there was still today.

Often I think about getting even for myself or one of my teammates who was blasted insensible, but that's not the purpose of the game. Sure I think about Mansfield hitting me with a cheap shot, but I'm not going into the game looking to break his neck. It still comes back to the fact that if Lynn Swann runs across the middle, he's liable to get hit again. Only next time I'll be watching Big Brother a little more closely, too.

Dressing for a game, any game, is a ritual with me. I take great care with my shoes because they are im-

portant. I make sure my cleats are tight and new because I don't want to slip. Next, I put on two pairs of
socks and jam my foot into the shoe. I want a tight fit.
Then I tape my shoes on tight. This way there is no
chance of my shoe giving way under the stress of starting
and stopping. I believe that every ounce of running
power can be generated into my body. It seems to make
for an explosive start and maximum speed on contact.

Of course, I take care with other articles of equipment, but I stress taping my wrists and forearms. I use
rolls of tape on my wrists and forearms for protection,
and the tape gives a more solid feel during contact.

After all the gear is on and I'm taped, I channel all
my attention to the game and the people I'll be going
up against.

There are passive teams in the NFL that try to win
with pure execution rather than aggressive and violent
play. Execution has a place in the NFL, but unfortunately passive teams usually lose while physical teams
usually win. That is simply the basic rule of football
or any contact sport. In any contact sport it behooves
the athlete to be physical.

The Vikings, Browns, and Bengals are just a few of
the passive teams that can hang in there for a quarter
or two against the heavyweights, but in the end pain and
punishment have a way of warping their will to win.
I've played against the nonphysical teams, and for a
few quarters it was a respectable game. But when the
final gun went off, the Raiders usually won.

When playing against a passive team, one hit, a good
hit, will usually discourage the entire offensive team
from getting fancy. I mean that if the linemen open up
a big hole and the running back picks up some good
yardage but in the process gets severed from reality, it
all has a way of demoralizing the entire offensive team
and picking up the defense. It might be hard to accept,
but even in professional football there are some individuals and even teams that back down from brutal contact.
I don't like that type of game, because I have a tendency
to let down a little myself. I realize that my paycheck
is dependent on my ability to inflict a demoralizing

punishment to the opponent, but still, in a passive semi-contact game, I get sloppy.

However, the Pittsburgh Steelers are far from passive and they are not easily intimidated. Then again the Raiders have a reputation for being a rather surly bunch that thrives on brutal contact themselves. When two football giants such as the Steelers and Raiders get together, there isn't any backing down on either side.

When playing in a big game against a physical team such as the Steelers, I look for individual keys in the personality of the athletes in the primary positions. I realize that the Steelers as a whole will not be intimidated any more than will the Raiders. I accept that fact and look to channel my aggression directly toward the weaker athletes on the team. Sometimes in an important physical game little things, such as a dropped pass or a running back slipping down short of the first down, will mean the difference between a win or a loss.

Several years ago we were playing Miami in a very important game. During the first half we were doubling Paul Warfield, the Dolphins All-Pro wide receiver. Warfield is a great athlete and has a tendency to deliver the big play at the right time. My assignment in that particular game was to discourage him from attempting to make the big play against us. On a third down play Warfield bolted off the line of scrimmage and made a good outside move. Just as Nemo Wilson moved to cover him outside, Warfield cut back over the middle and was open by five yards. Bob Greise threw a perfect pass, but Paul caught more than just the ball. From my deep position I had nearly seven yards to build up my momentum and I caught Paul with a devastating shot in the ribs and throat. Warfield was scraped off the field unconscious. Later in the game, to my surprise, Paul Warfield returned to the action. At the time we were hanging on to a one-point lead, but the Dolphins were driving. On a critical fourth down play, Greise dropped back to pass and looked for Warfield, who by now had beaten Nemo again on a good out pattern. The ball was in flight, but just as it was to drop into Paul's hands, he turned and looked for me. Well, I was there and I caught him in the back with a pretty good shot. Warfield dropped the ball, one that he usually would have caught easily, and the Dolphins lost the game.

Under normal conditions Warfield could have caught that pass one hundred times in a row. But playing against the Raiders, Paul found himself in a different situation. For a split second Paul Warfield lost his concentration. In that little period of mental lapse, my physical presence had paved the way for his mistake. Whenever I can get a receiver or running back worried about me, his concentration is finished and I will win.

With the Steelers, I look for these particular areas to channel my violence through. I must be brutal, but legal, because infractions of the rules and the resultant penalties only tend to hurt the defense rather than help it. My object against the Steelers is to find their weak links and move from there but still respect the rules of the game.

The Pittsburgh Steelers have balance. The offensive team can move the ball while the defensive team is, at times, impossible to beat. However, I don't analyze the Steelers on paper and look for the weakness that way. I have analyzed the Steelers by playing against them, and the experience of battle has made me a wiser player. For example, on paper Franco Harris is big, fast, and devastating as a running back. On paper his stats look good, but in reality Franco is a big man who will sometimes back down. If Franco had the aggressiveness of a Gayle Sayers, Jimmy Brown, Walter Payton, Earl Campbell, or a hundred or more great running backs, his achievements would be unequalled. But Franco runs from sideline to sideline instead of aggressively straight ahead. Some coaches may argue that Franco is concerned with his personal safety and runs with his particular style for self-preservation. From my point of view a running back is paid to carry the ball forward, and if that means running through, over, or around the defense, he ought to make the effort. Franco either runs for the sidelines when it gets a bit sticky or he gives way to one of his patented slips.

Therefore, Franco becomes a target for me and the entire Raider defense. We know that by pounding him hard and often Franco's will to win is going to be warped. It may not be important, but then again the ballgame could rest on Franco's courage. I've seen Franco against less physical teams just blast away for those third down and short yardage plays and I've seen him slip and fall down short of the first down on similar plays against the more physical teams. It pays to get physical with running backs and receivers.

Lynn Swann, although a great receiver, lacks consistency on patterns over the middle. Against some teams he runs a sharp quick pattern, but against the Raiders he rounds everything off and looks for openings in the zone rather than making those bold dashes across the middle.

I can't fault these people for playing their style of football, because in their own way they may be right. Franco has been around many years and has seemed to avoid serious injuries. Lynn Swann is still doing a great job, and also trying to keep himself out of the hospital. It's all a matter of style, but nonetheless, it remains an area for me to exploit once the whistle starts the game.

The game itself started the way I figured—violent and brutal. When playing against the Steelers or any of the physical teams, one comes to expect solid contact and flaring tempers, but somehow this game immediately started getting out of hand. Early in the game our wide receiver, Cliff Branch, caught a short turn-in pass and was quickly scooped up by Steeler defensive back, Mel Blount. Cliff isn't a very physical receiver, and when Mel had him shackled, that should have been the end of the play. Unfortunately, it wasn't. Instead of just making the tackle, Mel grabbed Cliff, turned him upside down, and then tried to pile-drive his head into the ground. It was obviously a deliberate attempt to hurt the man and it got some of our defensive people talking about getting the Steelers' receivers. Personally, I don't believe in the big brother routine. I don't like to see a man like Blount, or anyone for that matter, try to maim a fellow player and friend, but it still does not warrant my going after one of the Steelers' receivers. However, an event such as Blount's hit does adversely affect the mood of the game because some individuals are going to get mad and start taking other cheap shots.

Before long it became more serious than Mel Blount putting a little extra into his shots. Both teams started. On a dive play, a Steeler tight end, Randy Grossman, hit me after the whistle. I defended myself by throwing Grossman to the ground and punching him. I was mad, and it was just a reaction and not a premeditated act, but I ended up on the short end of a penalty flag. Naturally, I protested the call, but the officials didn't listen. My point was that Grossman hit me late, and the films bear testimony to that fact. I don't believe that Randy's hit was a deliberate infraction of the rules, but I still resented the shot. When I fought back I became the villain. I realize two wrongs can never make a right, but in the heat of an important battle tempers are going to fire up. It was wrong that I punched Grossman, but during the tension of an important game, an athlete reacts erratically. I just think the official should have used more judgment in the call. After all, under normal conditions I don't punch and kick my opponent. The official should have realized that something serious had caused the incident, but it just didn't work out that way.

I should have guessed that the officiating was only going to become more one-sided as the game continued. After all, Mel Blount had hit Cliff with a cheap shot and there wasn't a flag. Grossman had hit me late, and no flag. Then I fire back with a natural reaction and it's fifteen yards against the Raiders.

Later in the game the Steelers were driving for a touchdown. Franco took the ball and tried the middle. There wasn't a hole, so I knew he would either fall down or run for the sidelines. Since the last few attempts on Franco's part had been no-gain slips in the backfield, he moved outside and made a straight path for the sidelines. I had a good angle, and Franco was going to get busted before he reached safety. He realized that fact, too, and before I could get within five yards of him, Franco slipped and fell to the ground. I was mad. Damn! If a man is going to put on a uniform and play football, he should at least play it like a man. Under the NFL rules a ball carrier isn't officially down until a defender either has made the tackle or has physically touched and downed a man. Franco still had the chance to get up and run because no defensive man had yet touched him. I realized that Franco wasn't going to attempt to get up and I really wanted to blast into him. I wanted to stick my helmet in his ribs or face or anything. I just wanted to hit him, but instead I lazily downed him with a light slap on his helmet. I didn't give the incident a second thought until I got up and saw the penalty flag. Once again I was a villain. The official felt that I had hit Franco too hard and he flagged me for unnecessary roughness. That was a ridiculous call! I wasn't even moving half-speed when I fell over Franco, and I had slapped at him open-handed with more of a disgusted effort than anything else, but still, I was hit with a fifteen yard penalty. It happens that way, though. Sometimes you get on the wrong side of an official and he drops the flag every chance he gets. It's not fair, but it's still part of the game.

Shortly after that penalty the Steelers tried a sweep to my side. I had the outside responsibility and as I started to move into position I spotted Rocky Bleier coming at me from the blind side. He was coming low, going for my knee. Ever since last season and Ray Mansfield's shot at my knee, I've been sensitive about those cheap shots. I reacted. I know that Bleier was surprised when I turned quickly and blasted him with a fist and forearms up under his face mask. Standing over Rocky I glared down and said, "I don't like people getting into my knees." Rocky is tough and man enough to know that if the situation had been reversed, he would have blasted me to protect his knees. He jumped up and said, "No problem," and ran back to the Steelers' huddle. I looked around to see whether or not another flag had been thrown, but the man with the stripes had missed this one. I guess if the official is a poor enough one to make mistakes on the flags he throws, he can miss a legitimate call, too.

Later the Steelers tried the same play, but Rocky Bleier wasn't in my area. This time I spotted Lynn Swann nonchalantly roaming over the middle, and I drew a bead on his rib cage. But then I saw George

Atkinson homing in on Lynn, and with one quick swipe of a forearm, George sort of pulled Lynn down using a club-like action across the head and side of the neck. Lynn went down and George moved in toward the ball carrier. The shot to Swann was by no means an over-powering one. In fact, I thought that it had simply caught Lynn off guard and he had lost his balance. But Lynn needed some assistance getting off the field. The entire incident was, at the time, so insignificant that George wasn't even credited with a "knockout" or even a "limp-off." It was nothing, absolutely nothing. While the action was going on, I could see Lynn running back and forth behind the Steelers' bench.

Shortly thereafter the Steelers scored a go-ahead touchdown, making the score 21–14. It had been that kind of day. One team would score and then the other team would score.

On the next series the Steelers stopped us cold and had the ball again. When their offensive unit came out on the field, Swann stayed behind and ran lazy pat-terns behind the bench. He seemed perfectly healthy, and I wondered why he wasn't in the game. Then, on the first play, I got John Stallworth. Stallworth caught the ball over the middle and a split second later, I hit him hard. As a result of the contact, John twisted his knee and had to be helped off the field. George gave me credit for a "limp-off." Now, when Lynn Swann was called up and told to go back into the game, he collapsed on the sidelines. One second he was perfectly normal and the next second he was supposedly out cold. It could be that it took George's shot a long time to register, but then again, I really wonder.

Even without Swann and Stallworth, the Steelers went in for another score and built their lead to 28–14. Bradshaw had a great time running up and down the sidelines showing the ball to the Raider fans. Evidently, Terry thought the game was over even though there were still over five minutes on the clock. Unfortunately for Bradshaw and the entire Steeler team, five minutes were more than enough for us to come back.

When Kenny Stabler got his hands on the football, he started performing feats of magic. Within a minute the scoreboard was lighting up and now read, Steelers 28, Raiders 21.

We stopped the Steelers on their next series and they kept us in our own territory when we got the ball back. With a little more than three minutes to play, Coach Madden decided to kick the ball deep and ask the defense to come up with the big play. After three running plays the Steelers were faced with a fourth down and ten. Bobby Walden, the Steelers' punter, was rushed into a bad kick and once again Stabler was operating from good field position.

In a matter of seconds the game was tied at 28, but the Steelers were going to have another chance. After kicking deep, the Steelers took over on their own twenty and from there Bradshaw decided to try some magic of his own. One play later Terry Bradshaw made the ball disappear from the Steelers' offense. Actually, Bradshaw was under fire; he threw a wild pass into the strength of our secondary, and linebacker Willie Hall made a great interception. From there we ran a few running plays to use up the time and then kicked a last second field goal.

The game was over and the Raiders won, 31–28. It's strange that professional football players can be brutal enemies during the contest but once the final gun sounds, the animosities are usually over. Everyone realized it had been a great game and even a greater come-from-behind win. In a semiserious tone some of the Steelers warned us that they would return for the play-offs later in the year. Actually, there was a lot of truth in that statement because the Raiders and Steelers usually do meet in the play-off games. In all, I would say that most of the players left the field pretty good friends, in spite of everything that had happened. Naturally, I thought it was a good game, a great game, but there was always next week to start considering.

Early Monday morning I received a call from my attorney, Tony DeCello. Tony lives in Pittsburgh, a strange place for me to have an attorney, but that's the way it worked out. Anyway, Tony called and asked, "Tate, did you hear the news?"

"Damn, Tony, what time it is?" I asked. "It's still dark."

Tony told me it was eight o'clock in the morning . . . Pittsburgh time. That meant it was five o'clock in Oakland.

For my attorney to call me at five in the morning meant that something serious must have happened. As he was telling me the story, I started to wake up. I didn't understand everything the first time so I asked Tony to run it by me again. He said, "Tate, Lynn Swann is in the hospital with a serious concussion and Chuck Noll is blasting the hell out of you and George. Noll is claiming that there are 'criminal elements' in professional football. The Commissioner has already called my office and they are going to take legal action—fines, I think."

Well, I still couldn't make heads or tails out of the situation. First of all, I hadn't touched Swann in the game. I was looking for him, but he never came anywhere near me. And the "criminal element" talk I simply couldn't understand.

"Tony," I said, "Call me later. I'm going back to sleep."

That was how serious I thought the situation was. I didn't know what was going on, and quite frankly I didn't care. Commissioner Pete Rozelle has the right to sound off. After a tough game I need my sleep, and that was much more important to me than another publicity stunt.

Later in the morning George Atkinson called me and laughed about Chuck Noll's comments. George said, "Tate, the coach in Pittsburgh has referred to you and me as criminals and he wants us put in jail."

At the time I still had no idea of the impact the game and the accusations were having on the public. I thought that it wasn't serious because nothing had really happened. But as the day went on, I began to realize that a few isolated incidents were getting blown up by the press, Steeler coach Chuck Noll, and Commissioner Pete Rozelle.

Later that afternoon I found out that Lynn Swann really was in the hospital with a concussion. I had seen

George hit Swann and at the time it didn't look that serious. After all, even after the hit, I had seen Lynn running up and down the sidelines apparently in fairly good health, but somewhere between Oakland and Pittsburgh he had evidently developed a serious concussion. Regardless of Swann's condition, I still couldn't figure out why my name was dragged into the mess. After all, I didn't hit Swann. I remembered that last year when I got Swann, Chuck Noll had made the statement that I should be barred from ever playing football in the NFL, but that was last year.

It took some time, but all parts of the puzzle started falling into place. I found out that Rocky Bleier—the same Rocky Bleier who had taken a shot at my knee during our miraculous win over the Steelers—had written a letter to Commissioner Rozelle regarding my tactics. In the letter, which I later read, I was accused of willfully trying to hurt receivers and running backs. In addition, I was accused of being a cheap-shot artist and of employing tactics designed to seriously injure my opponents. The letter also implied that many players feared for their lives when playing against me and that some type of disciplinary action should be taken immediately.

There were rumors that other Steelers had written the Commissioner complaining about my style. My first reaction was, "Where's Franco's letter?" But I soon found out he never sent one in. To say the least, I was surprised. But a greater surprise was the shock I felt about Rocky Bleier being part of such trash. Rocky has a certain amount of courage and he knows about the game. More important than all that, he knows why I fought back against him. Sure, I go out and use the Hook and I hit hard, but it's all part of the game. Given the same opportunity, any player would try to blast me into the nickel stands, too. The point is that my job is based upon my ability to be intimidating and violent. Yet my every action is well within the structure of the NFL rules. If and when the rules change, I'll change my style. But for now, I prevent the opposition from scoring by destroying their confidence. A running back cannot run toward the goal line and away from me at the same time. Likewise, a receiver cannot concentrate on catching a pass while listening for my footsteps.

I have never faulted Rocky for running too fast or blocking too hard, because I realize why he is paid. Randy Grossman is said to have a great pair of hands and can catch anything near him. Should I cry because Grossman can make great catches? Or maybe I should look into the physical aspects of playing tight end? Okay, Grossman is a down lineman. He can catch a pass or he can come down the field and block. There is no rule that tells Grossman how fast he can run or how hard he can block. If his jobs calls for coming at me full speed and knocking me over hard and violently, and he does it, then fine. I accept that as part of the game. Playing free safety is a job of hitting and getting hit. I've been hit by linemen who outweigh me by eighty or ninety pounds. When one of those beasts hits you straight on or from the blind side while moving full speed, it hurts! I literally bounce along the ground after getting smacked by an offensive guard or tackle but I still realize it's all part of the game. I have never cried about anyone hitting me too hard or getting blind-sided, because it's a chance I take every time I suit up to play football. Even when Mansfield speared me in the championship game of 1975 and my knee was injured, I didn't complain. Even when I was hit in Denver's Mile High Stadium after the play was over with a cheap shot that cost me knee surgery, I didn't complain.

I cannot stress enough the fact that football is a violent and brutal game. When people start pounding each other, they bleed. When running backs moving full speed slam into defensive people, bones often break and men find themselves severed from reality. Look into the basic objective of a football game and you'll see what I mean. An offensive team is put on the field and given the responsibility to move the ball forward and score points. But a defensive team is also out there trying to counteract every offensive move. The human body was not designed with a football game in mind, but nonetheless this type of violence seems to satisfy a psychological need of our society. The Romans had the gladiators, hungry lions, and Christians; and we have boxing, hockey, and football.

Whenever I step onto the field for a game, I expect to get knocked around, and I consider the possibility I will sustain a serious injury. If I get hit and injured, whether by a clean block or a cheap shot, I just consider it part of the game. I know that in the heat of battle there are going to be individuals who let their emotions get the best of them, and from time to time I'll get hit late or clipped. But it doesn't mean I have to cry to the press about criminals in football, and it certainly doesn't require a letter to the Commissioner. I get hit and I hit because it's part of football. Sometimes the hits will be late or questionable, but it happens. I guess that's why we have rules and officials—just to make sure everyone gets busted up according to the book. Fast running, great catches, hard hits, late hits, and cheap shots are all just part of the game, and I don't believe any rules of the Commissioner can control these areas of football. Any time you put two or more athletes together and let them engage in a contact sport, tempers will flare and violence will prevail. When you consider that on a typical play during a football game twenty-two men, at the combined weight of better than two tons, engage in violent physical actions against each other, it's really no wonder that the game is brutal. Any athlete in the NFL who expects something less than brutality is thinking like a fool or hiding from reality.

Lynn Swann has great natural athletic ability. Swann can leap high and make great catches, and he has the speed and quickness to beat you long or short. But when it comes to hitting or getting hit, Lynn has a tendency to shy away. I would expect him to write the Commissioner a letter, but I never imagined that Grossman and Bleier would do such a thing. I was certain I had done nothing wrong, but because of letters to the Commissioner and several questionable calls, I was faced with a problem. Public opinion was being manipulated against my style of play.

Even though Howard Cosell dedicated a half-time show on "Monday Night Football" to George and me, the Commissioner's office would only state that action would be taken in the near future. According to Cosell, George and I were worse than the Prince of Darkness himself but we both felt that the validity of any statement Cosell made would be questionable at best. The show and the comments were simply a part of Cosell's plan to build sensationalism into a small part of a football game while portraying himself as the crusader against violence and brutality in football. Football is a violent and brutal game, but for the news media to devote any time to cheap shots and cheap-shot artists is absurd. Still, though, all the undesirable publicity did have a bad effect on George and me. Every time we came anywhere near contact, the officials started throwing penalty flags for unnecessary roughness. In a game against New England several weeks after the Swann incident, George and I attempted to bring down their running back, Jess Philips. Several years before, Jess and been a Raider, and we knew back then he was a very difficult man to tackle. Neither George nor I made a good hit, and Jess was bucking and dragging us along for extra yardage. Finally, I got in a position to flip him and slam him to the ground. The official immediately threw a flag. It was ridiculous, and everyone knew it. When George protested, the official threw another flag, and on a play that started out to be a six-yard gain, the officials helped to make it a quick thirty-six yards. Even Jess jumped up and asked the official, "Man, what the hell are you doing? There wasn't anything cheap about that shot. What gives, anyway?"

Even the man who was getting hit and knocked to the ground thought it was a quick and unjustifiable call, but the official said, "Tatum, I'm not going to let you get away with a damn thing. I'm watching you all the way!"

During another game I was clipped, and the official was standing right on the spot watching the play. Naturally, I asked the official about the clip, and he replied, "I'm not watching anyone except you."

Most of the players and coaches know and understand about the game, but once in a while someone will come along who cries and complains loud enough and long enough until the news media listens. When that happens, it becomes one uphill struggle to prove your point. I am not a cheap player. I hit hard, but I've never taken an illegal shot at anyone. Sure, I've caught receivers close to the sidelines, but never out-of-bounds. It's also true that I used the Hook, but the technique was legal then. It might sound strange, but there is a legal and an illegal way to use the Hook. Using a straight forearm and swinging it into a player is illegal, but I would keep my arm in tight against my body. I would attempt to strip the ball from the offensive man while at the same time trying to catch his head in between my biceps and forearms. Believe me, it was legal, and what's more, the Hook was always the best intimidator in the business. I've probably used the Hook at one time or another on every receiver and running back in the NFL. Every time I've been called on the carpet by the Commissioner, the tactic was never questioned. So the Hook was legal, and until the rules were rewritten I stung people with that particular technique.

I guess it was several weeks later that I actually received a certified letter from Pete Rozelle stating that I was being fined $750. The letter explained that because I punched Grossman, slapped Franco, and slugged Bleier, the Commissioner deemed it necessary to fine me $250 for each incident. I wasn't about to pay the fines and demanded a hearing. By shelling out $750 to the NFL, I would have been giving in to the worst kind of autocracy. I have never believed that the Commissioner has the right to set fines without hearings, and I filed a formal protest.

Even if I had been wrong about those three incidents, I still would have refused to pay the fines because of my right to have a hearing. The truth of the matter was that I did slug Grossman after being provoked, but the Franco Harris incident was absurd. If they wanted to penalize me for anything, then drop the flag because of the Bleier hit and step off fifteen yards. If the Commissioner intended to start fining every player because of action during the game then we might just as well hang up the gear and start playing ping-pong.

If Rozelle felt the fines were justifiable, then let him

prove it through his attorneys and make me pay the money.

Rozelle accepted the challenge and arranged a date that fit into our schedule. After a Sunday game in New England, which we lost 48–17, I flew into New York for a Monday morning hearing. Using game films, Pete tried to prove that I was guilty of infractions. When he started with the Grossman incident, the films proved that Randy hit me late. Still, the Commissioner contended that I had punched and kicked a man. Next he tried to get me on the Franco Harris slap, but the films proved that I had the right to hit the man. More than just hit or slap at Franco, I could have blasted into him without mercy. At that point the score seemed to be even at 1–1, but the Commissioner came up with the Bleier movies and I openly admitted my guilt during that particular play. I tried to bring up the previous season when Mansfield injured my legs and explain that I was sensitive about low crack back blocks, but the man just wasn't listening. I felt as though the walls were closing in on me. I was in a hostile environment, and regardless of the facts, I was to be guilty as charged.

Although the news media seemed to know and understand everything about the "criminal element" incident, quite frankly, I didn't. Even after my hearing with Pete Rozelle, I knew little or nothing about the deal. First of all, there were, as I explained, three separate charges against me: Franco, Grossman, and Bleier. At the hearing Rozelle said that the charges were "unnecessary roughness," and then he said that I had acted "unprofessionally." Pete Rozelle and his lawyers were vague about everything.

Next, I was shown the famous letters, but wasn't permitted copies. I was just told to read the letters from the Steelers, and when my attorney asked for copies the answer was a polite "No!" To me the hearing had shades of the Old West. The bad guy was in the courtroom at his hearing while the hangman was knotting the rope securing it over the nearest tree.

Of course, we looked at game films, but they only proved my incident with Grossman was provoked by Grossman, that Franco actually hadn't been down, and the hit on Rocky could have been passed off as part of the game or maybe my bending the rules. But in all, the entire hearing was so damn vague that I was upset for several days. I believe that in view of the Atkinson-Swann action, the NFL felt that Jack Tatum's name should be mentioned, too. But that's the kind of ink in the paper I'm trying to get away from.

I'm getting a little ahead of myself, but much later Pete Rozelle sent down a $500 fine for my "unnecessary roughness" charges. Evidently, Pete felt a little compassion for me and reduced my sentence by $250. But that's not the issue or the point. I wasn't guilty of unnecessary roughness or unsportsmanlike conduct. I was a victim of the system and resented it. I resented even more the fact that Rozelle wasn't interested in my side of the story. The verdict was in and I was guilty regardless of favorable evidence or the NFL's lack of proof that a crime had been committed.

As I flew back to Oakland I started thinking about my life and how dramatically it had changed from farm boy in North Carolina to "paid assassin" for the Oakland Raiders. While deep in thought about those early years, I began to realize that someone was staring at me. As I looked across the aisle I saw a young boy looking back expressionlessly.

"What's happenin', Pal?" I asked.

He never answered the question. The kid just sat there looking at me. "Are you going for a vacation in California or do you live there?" I asked, trying to get the little dude going.

Then this little man's mother said, "Tell Mr. Tatum that you live in Oakland and you watch all his football games."

Well, this little fellow wouldn't say a word. He just sat there and stared, but his mother and I started talking. She said, "We've seen you play on television and at the stadium. You know, we are Oakland Raider fans."

It was small talk, but a nice conversation. Finally, the lady got around to saying, "You know, I've pictured you much differently. I guess when you put on your equipment and play in a game you have to be a different personality. I half expect all football players to be brutes in real life but you're real people, too."

Just then the little dude said, "Jack, can I have your autograph? You're my favorite player. You wear number thirty-two in the games but how's come on my bubble gum card you wear number thirty-one?"

I signed the little man an autograph first and then said, "Come over here and sit beside me. Now, let me tell you the story about my rookie year and why I was number thirty-one."

3

IN THE GHETTO

I would have been perfectly content to have spent my childhood listening to my grandfather, Wesley Starr, telling me stories of the great Civil War. With a particular fondness I remember Grandpa telling me how he and General Grant, riding white chargers, sent a hundred or more Johnny Rebs fleeing for their lives. I'd sit for hours on hours beneath the green tapestry of a willow tree as Grandpa rambled on about the Great War and many other actual events in history on which he had had a direct bearing. Why, Grandpa even told me that he had helped row General Washington across the Delaware on a winter's night in the first war he ever fought.

Grandpa Starr had a way of painting stories with simple words that could mesmerize a young boy, but as I grew older and much more knowledgeable, it began to seem that the old gentleman had a tendency to exaggerate a little. For if he and Grant actually did send those rebels fleeing, and if in fact he did row Washington across the Delaware, then my grandfather was remarkably well-preserved for a man closing in on two hundred years of life. I learned much later that Grandpa was a sharp-witted gentleman of some sixty odd years who had a fancy for history. However, it had still been a delightful experience for a young barefoot country boy to sit in the shade on those hot summer days and be whisked away by the magic of an old man's words to exciting eras of history.

I was born in Crouse, North Carolina, on November 18, 1948. My early childhood memories are filled with a special contentment because my early life encompassed the peaceful Carolina countryside and those fantastic journeys of the mind I made while listening to Grandpa. With all this, and good food, a roof overhead, and parents that loved me, what more could a little boy really expect?

In those early years I never actually sat down and thought about my future, but I'm sure if a decision were to have been made, I probably would have trotted off over the countryside with my Grandpa and gone into the next battle he and Grant, or Washington, or even Patton were planning. Then again, maybe I would have just sat in the shade and waited for Grandpa to return and let him tell me about the fighting. My experiences in Crouse typified the lazy half-asleep movements of the humid and sticky South. Unlike most young boys, I had no ambition of growing up and becoming a cowboy or fireman. I guess I would have been perfectly content to just remain a happy child who vicariously rushed into adventure through a journey of the mind.

When I was nearing six years of age, my parents started talking about moving to New Jersey. Some of our relatives, my mother's brother Jim and his family, had left the South several years ago and found New Jersey to their liking. When they wrote about the higher paying jobs and better school systems in the North, my parents grew more serious about moving.

North Carolina suited my style of life, and I just wasn't interested in moving anywhere. After all, my father had a good job as a welder, and our home was comfortable and always filled with the scent of good things cooking. The idea of a better paying job for my father and better schools for us children just did not stimulate my interest. But nonetheless the rumors of a move to New Jersey persisted. We were a family of seven, but democracy did not exist within the structure of the Tatum household. Although my parents, Lewis and Annie Mae, were quite set on moving up to New Jersey, my two brothers, Manuel and Samuel, along with my two sisters, Peggy and Mabel, protested against the idea. I was the youngest, and for the most part, not expected to understand the intricacies of moving to another state, but I still filed my protest along with my older sisters and brothers.

Instead of taking a vote about whether or not we were actually going to move, my father simply sat us down and explained his decision without even considering the unanimous disapproval of his five children. He informed us that we were making the move to New Jersey and anyone that didn't like the idea could stay behind with my mother's parents, Delzora and Wesley Starr. I remember thinking that was all quite fine with me and quickly decided to tell my parents, "Have a nice trip and come back and visit with me sometime."

But just as I began to wonder how much I would miss my parents, I heard my dad say, "That applies to everyone except John David and Mabel." I was John David, and Mabel was the youngest of my sisters. "You two are just kids and can't take on the responsibility of caring for yourselves," my father went on to explain.

There were times when my father's voice had the ring of authority to it, and those were the times you never said, "But, Daddy. . . ." You learned early in life when a subject wasn't open for discussion. Mabel and I realized that Samuel, Manuel, and Peggy would be staying behind while the rest of us would be heading north into a new adventure.

The imagination of a six-year-old boy can be fantastic. It was always quite easy for me to picture in my mind the stories Grandpa had told, and now I was letting that same imagination run to New Jersey. I envisioned new friends, naturally, but I also anticipated as my new swimming hole a quiet lake shimmering in the sunshine. I further imagined a river lined with green and golden trees and a small, but rather nice-looking, pier that jutted out over the exact spot where a school of catfish spent their time just waiting to be caught by a little boy like me. There were some bass and a few trout, too. "Yes," I thought, "New Jersey will be a nice place." I carried those nice thoughts and visions into my sleep as the night fell and my father drove ever northward.

As morning broke, the reality of Paterson, New Jersey, slapped me to consciousness. I peered out the window of our car at gaunt stacks belching the black smoke and soot that was falling over the crowded tenement dwellings. The cotton land of Carolina had been traded for a maze of chipped concrete, broken glass, and a serrated mass of towers and spires standing silently against a faded red sky. I was scared and already longing for my home.

We moved in with Uncle Jim and Aunt Billie Starr. My aunt and uncle had a small but quite nice home in Paterson. I must admit that with my two cousins, Leon (he was the oldest) and Rayvon (he was my age), and the five of us, plus Uncle Jim and Aunt Billie, it was very crowded. We all managed to live together and get along, but I do believe sanity prevailed only because everyone knew that as soon as my dad found work, we would move into our own place.

Rayvon was a blessing for me in my attempts at justifying the move from Crouse to Paterson. It was quite obvious that Paterson was different from Crouse and if not for Rayvon, I would have had great difficulty in adjusting to my new world. There were plenty of kid things to do around Paterson. We could go down to the railroad yard and throw rocks at passing commuter trains or play in the wreckage and ruins of old buildings. I wasn't opposed to throwing rocks, but aiming at trains bothered me. After taking me to the railroad yard, Rayvon said, "I like to throw rocks but it's not much fun hitting the train." We both agreed that someone could get hurt. More than the chance of one of the passengers on the train getting hurt, Rayvon and I considered the possibility of getting caught. Then, for sure, someone would get hurt, and in all probability, it would be two little dudes named John David and Rayvon. After a couple days of throwing rocks at the trains I asked, "Rayvon, why do we have to do this?" He answered, "Because everyone does." Although we were young, the reason behind "everyone does" wasn't strong enough to keep us at the railroad yard. There were other things to do, and we went on to explore the rest of the city.

Playing in the wreckage and ruins of the old buildings wasn't bad except for the warning Uncle Jim had issued when we first arrived. Uncle Jim said, "Rayvon, if you take J. D. down by those old buildings and I catch ya', I'll beat the hell out of both of you."

The buildings were ideal for our war games, but Uncle Jim's warnings constantly rang somewhere in the deep chambers of my mind. With each passing day, the excitement of climbing around the piles of bricks, broken glass, and rusted-out pipes caused us to forget Uncle Jim's threats, and the old buildings became our playground. I was particularly fond of exploring the condemned buildings with rotted-out flooring and weak and creaky staircases. When we would carry our war games into one of those old buildings, it would sometimes take hours to sight the enemy. But I learned to listen for the sound of a floorboard creaking under the weight of the enemy and then plan my attack.

After several weeks of playing and exploring the old buildings, Uncle Jim's warnings faded completely from my mind. In the evenings, when he would fix himself a drink from his bottle of I. W. Harper, Uncle Jim would usually ask, "What did you boys do today?" Rayvon or I would answer, "Nothin' special, just played outside." Every so often he would ask, "You guys don't play in the old buildings, do you?" Rayvon and I would both answer, "Oh no, a kid could get hurt down there."

Well, we were right about a kid getting hurt down there. Unfortunately, our fears about a kid getting hurt even more when he got home were also correct. One day Rayvon went through a rotted area of flooring. One second he was on the fourth floor moving in on me (I was hiding in a closet), and the next thing I knew, Rayvon screamed, fell through the flooring, and landed on the third floor. My first reaction was to run downstairs and shoot him with my gun made from a rusted pipe, but then I realized he could be hurt, seriously hurt. I yelled in terror and ran down the stairs to help him. When I reached Rayvon, he was lying face down over a pile of splintered boards and dusty plaster. I stood frozen with fear as terrible images flashed through my mind. He could have broken his neck, or legs, or even had a piece of sharp floor board sticking in his side. I felt weak with anxiety as I approached Rayvon's motionless body. Then Rayvon whirled over and said, "Bam, you're dead!" He got me, but that wasn't the end of the battle. Rayvon had actually hurt himself. He had cut and twisted his leg and had bruises all over his body, head, and face. He got me, but when we got home, Uncle Jim got him. That day ended our war games in the old buildings forever, but it was still a big city with other areas to explore.

We tried playing the games that other kids in our neighborhood played, but it wasn't much fun. Most of the other kids thought stealing things from the stores in the area was great fun and a true test of one's manhood. Sometimes they stole items they could use or eat, but usually it was a game of stealing for the sake of stealing, and I just couldn't understand it at all. Actually, I couldn't even understand stealing food and things you could use, because I realized that someone was going to have to pay for the merchandise in the long run. One time Rayvon and I went into a small grocery store. The plan was for Rayvon to keep the storekeeper busy while I sneaked around to a side aisle and stole something. I was trying to keep an eye on Rayvon and the storekeeper and at the same time grab something off the shelf. We were smooth and I slipped out the door with a big box tucked under my shirt. I ran around the corner and started to laugh with relief. Seconds later Rayvon ran out of the store and we beat it on down the road. After running several blocks, we were sure it was cool to check out the merchandise. Rayvon said, "Wow, J. D., that's a big box you got under your shirt, what didya' get?"

"I don't know," was my reply. I tugged out the box and we both stood there and looked. "What is it J. D.? What's it used for?" Rayvon asked me.

Hell, I didn't know, and since neither of us could read, we tried to figure it out. Rayvon felt that maybe these pads were used for cleaning cars or something like that but I figured they were for shining shoes. Except for the fact that they were white and thick, they did look very much like the cloths the shoeshine boys used. We both eventually agreed that they were for shining shoes and decided to do a good deed. The plan was to go home and shine everyone's shoes. At the time I couldn't figure it out, but when my aunt came home and saw us shining shoes with those pads, she became a little uptight. Rayvon and I figured that she had found out we stole the pads, and when she asked, "What are you guys doing?" Rayvon screamed out, "Don't hit me! J. D. stole 'em!"

Throwing rocks at trains wasn't my bag, and after the incident at the building, I realized there must be a safer way to spend the summer. Then, when my father explained why a person doesn't steal, I understood that the life of crime could be a painful experience. There just had to be something else for us to do. When we sat around the house complaining that there wasn't anything to do, Aunt Billie found a few things to keep us busy. Washing windows, dusting tables, cleaning the cellar, working in the yard . . . after a day or so of her idea of fun and games, Rayvon and I moved out into the streets again in search of other adventures.

Before long, my father found work and we moved. Then we moved again and again. In the space of three months, we had moved four times and were planning yet another move. These moves were spurred by different reasons: one because of better housing in another section of town; another because of a different job my father found; but regardless, it was becoming a difficult life. I would get settled in school, make a few friends, and the next day we would move to another area of Paterson. Then the moves involved greater distances. Instead of moving around Paterson, my father found a job in Clifton, and we moved. After a few months in Clifton, my parents realized the rent was too high and we moved back into Paterson. I was about eight or nine years old and had moved more times than I could remember.

After a few years, my father's work became more secure and we sort of settled down in one area. It was a tough neighborhood, but I honestly tried to mind my own business and keep out of trouble. I wasn't happy with our situation and even though it had been years since I left Crouse, I still had a strong desire to return to my true home. Because of my loneliness and longing for the countryside, I became shy and reserved. It wasn't that my grades in school were bad or anything like that, I just never said much and became a loner for the most part.

One morning on my way to school, several young neighborhood hoodlums mistook my reserved ways for cowardice. I guess you could say that we lived on the other side of the tracks because every morning on my way to school, I had to walk through an underpass as trains would steam and whistle their way overhead. To cross over the tracks above the underpass would be dangerous, and only a fool would try such a thing. The trains would speed by at fifty and sixty miles an hour and several people had been killed shortcutting over the tracks. My father only had to tell me once about the importance of the underpass, and I knew that if anyone ever caught me up on the tracks, either the trains or my father would kill me. So walking to and from school through the underpass was a daily ritual for me.

That particular morning I was jumped by these two young hoods just as I came out of the underpass. They roughed me up a little and then the biggest one said, "Hey man, we own the underpass and any dude that uses it got to pay toll. Out with your milk money or we'll beat you."

They were both a little older than me and a little bigger, but I really wasn't scared. And to this day I don't know why I gave in to their demands, but I reached in my pocket and took out a dime. That was the money my dad had given me for milk and cookies, and the biggest one grabbed the dime and pushed me to the ground. They ran off laughing while I picked myself up and went on to school.

When it came time for our class to have a milk and cookie break, I sat back and watched the others enjoying themselves while I started to burn deep down inside.

I didn't like the idea of someone stealing from me. It not only hurt my feelings, but the more I thought about the incident, the more angry I became. I realized how the merchants felt when we stole from them. Although I was never what you would call an active thief, I still occasionally took little items that were not mine. That day I made a vow to never again take anything that wasn't mine from anyone. And by the same vow I wasn't going to treat with favor anyone that stole from me. I hoped the little thugs would never try me again. It hadn't been very enjoyable watching other kids eat cookies and drink milk, and I felt certain I would never let it happen again.

On my way out of the underpass the very next morning, I was accosted by the same two bullies, and once again I gave in to their demands. This time I felt more angry with myself than with the thugs because I had failed to live up to my vows. I needed a plan. My first alternative was to avoid any future confrontation. I started thinking about another route to school but I didn't want to get caught on the tracks by either a train or my father, so that was out of the question. I could have walked nine blocks or so in the other direction and crossed the tracks by using another underpass, but that would mean getting up at least forty-five minutes earlier in the morning. Being mugged two days in a row wasn't much fun, and there was always tomorrow morning, when I believed they would make it three. I had to do something. I knew I couldn't go to the police or anyone else for help, since squealing on anyone in my neighborhood was an unforgivable act of cowardice. My course of action was obviously to attack the attackers.

The next morning I found a piece of pipe about eighteen inches long. The pipe would more or less even up the odds. There were two of them, and now, two of me. As I walked through the underpass I hoped the thugs would not be there, because I really didn't want to hit anyone with that piece of pipe, but I certainly didn't relish the idea of being mugged every morning. "Maybe," I thought to myself, "just maybe they were satisfied and won't even be there today."

I also considered the possibility that I wouldn't be able to use the pipe and I pictured the two of them pounding little me into the ground and then stealing my dime. I even thought about turning around in the middle of the underpass and going over the tracks or even back home. But then I started thinking about my grandfather's stories and how he talked about bravery. "Sometimes," he would say, "sometimes a man has got to face danger. If he turns and runs, he isn't worth his weight in salt but if he fights for a cause, he's a man even if he loses the battle."

As I looked toward the far end of the underpass at the daylight I could see the silhouetted figures of the toll collectors. At that point, I made up my mind to face the danger and become a man.

When I reached the end of the tunnel, the biggest thug said, "Okay, fool, you know what to do next. Be out with the dime or I'll smack you in the mouth."

I reached inside my jacket for the security of the pipe tucked in my belt and said, "Kiss off, chump!"

There was a wavering in both of the little thugs' confidence, and they paused for a second. Then the biggest one reached out for me and I blasted him with the pipe. I hit him on the hand first and then started swinging wildly. I caught him with a good shot on the head, a couple times on the shoulder, and they both took off running and crying. I chased after the other one, too, and beat him a couple times on the back. As I chased them down the street, I could hear the small one screaming, "He's crazy! He's crazy!"

Well, crazy or not, I was never again asked to pay a toll at the end of the underpass, but there was another occasion when I had to prove my manhood. While I was growing up I had to prove myself only twice in fights. Actually, I consider piping the toll collectors only a matter of self-preservation, but there was one time in my early life that required a knockdown, drag-out fight. Of course, there were many fights in the ghetto, but for the most part, I was always able to bluff my way out. Most of the kids my age were scared to death of me for some reason, and I never had any problems with them. Once in a while some of the older guys would try to rough us up, but my confidence and assertiveness enabled me to bluff my way out of actually fighting. I wasn't afraid to fight, and it wasn't having to kick someone's teeth in or get mine kicked in that restrained me from being a street fighter. It was just that I always looked on fighting as a silly waste of energy.

And besides, more times than not, two dudes would get into a fight and seconds later they were buddies. So within my street gang I never had any serious problems. But one time the Crackers from the other side of the tracks came into our neighborhood looking for trouble. We found the Crackers or they found us, but regardless, we met in an alley face to face, getting ready to go at it. One of the Crackers made the statement, "Stanley Petrokoski can kick the hell out of any nigger in Niggertown."

The word "nigger" didn't bother me, but I didn't like the tone of his statement. I moved to the front and said, "I'm no nigger, but will a black do?"

All my friends were shocked to hear me pipe off like that because I wasn't the biggest member of the gang and I never started fights. Stanley pushed his way out of the crowd of Crackers and said, "You look like a nigger to me."

Stanley was big and I sort of stepped back a bit expecting one of the older stronger guys in our gang to jump in and accept the challenge. But Rayvon said, "Tate, he's talkin' to you. He just called you a nigger."

I had to choose whether to back down and be a coward or fight and get the hell beat out of me. Once again the voice of Grandpa Starr rang in my mind, and it came back to the point of being a man. Winning or losing the fight wasn't important, but proving yourself a man was what life was all about.

I fought and to my surprise, Stanley was a pussy. He was big and maybe even strong, but I was so damn fast that I sucker-punched him before he had a chance to blink. In all probability the fight was over after my first punch. Blood was gushing from around Stanley's mouth where his two front teeth had previously been and the light of confidence in his eyes had dulled to a fixed and stupid gaze, but I was riled up and decided to give Stanley a serious whipping. All the Crackers kept screaming, "Hit him, Stash, kick 'em, Stash," but Stash was getting punched up the alley toward the street. I admit that I didn't have to beat him so badly, but it was going to be a lesson no one would ever forget. My father and even my Uncle Jim used to say, "Don't start a fight, but if you've got to fight, then fight to beat the hell out of him." By the time we reached the street, Stanley's face was a mass of unfamiliar bumps and bruises. Somehow I got him up on my shoulder and threw him into the street in my final fit of rage. That was the last time I ever fought or had to bluff my way out of a fight while living in the ghetto. By the time my friends and the Crackers had finished adding to the story and developing my reputation as a ferocious fighter, I would have backed down from myself.

Street fighting was a common practice in the ghetto, but as I grew older and much wiser, I could never justify fighting. There was no purpose behind any of the fights I watched, and it all seemed a waste of time. To fight with someone because he was white, or black, or because he lived on the opposite side of town was utterly ridiculous. Fighting for self-preservation, or because you were a professional boxer, or maybe for the love of a woman had some merit, but street fights in the ghetto were ludicrous.

During the last half of my eighth year in school, my parents moved again. My father hadn't received a raise for several years and the rent on our apartment had tripled. We simply couldn't afford to live in the "classy" area of Paterson's ghetto so we moved into the bottom of Passaic's ghetto. This was a most difficult time for my family and myself but even under these extreme conditions, I tried to do the right things in life. I realized my parents had enough problems and I didn't want my actions to add to their growing list.

Passaic, New Jersey, or at least my part of Passaic, was a cluttered, noisy neighborhood. It was a belligerent environment that clamored with the noises of trains, factories, traffic, and kids playing in the street. When we had first moved to New Jersey everything at least looked respectable. Now that I was looking at my world through more mature eyes, I wanted out. Life to the residents of the Passaic ghetto was a deep, throbbing pain, and the escape routes from this world were marked with drugs and crime. Most of my friends became thieves, and worse, many others turned to hard drugs as their way out. I didn't want to live in a ghetto for the rest of my life, and I wanted something better for my parents, too. But there were times when I felt my world was a cell and we were all sentenced to life imprisonment.

I avoided trouble as though it were the plague, and my grades in school were good. Some of the guys in the neighborhood considered me strange because I was quiet and reserved and hardly ever went along with the gang's idea of fun and excitement. Occasionally, I would take a drink of wine and I did start to smoke, but that was it. I had a burning desire to get out of the ghetto, and I realized that education, not crime, was my ticket.

By the time I became a sophomore in high school, my physical abilities and size were impressive. Weighing 185 pounds and standing nearly five feet ten inches, no one ever questioned me or my ideas about getting out of the ghetto. I knew that my strength was natural and there wasn't anyone in the neighborhood that was stronger or faster. My once skinny arms had developed into solid ridges of muscle and my reflexes were unbelievably quick. Some people thought I would become a boxer, but I didn't have that type of desire. Then my Uncle Jim and my father started talking about football. I had always liked football and knew my skills in that game were far above average. In fact, most of the kids in the neighborhood didn't like to play tackle football against me. I was the fastest and hardest runner, and when I tackled, everyone (even the older guys) complained that I hit too hard. Until football practice started in our sophomore year, I had always considered myself abnormal. Something had to be wrong with me. It just wasn't normal to be the fastest, hardest running guy in town when most of the people I played against were much older and bigger. And when it came time to make tackles, I wasn't afraid, but actually enjoyed bone-crunching contact. Hard tackling involved something I couldn't figure out. Usually, there are two bodies involved in a tackle. When those two bodies collide, it seemed natural to assume that both would feel the effects of the shock, but when I'd hit someone, they usually didn't get up right away, and I would hardly feel a thing. It got to a point where I was becoming afraid of football. The contact had no effect on me, but I worried about what I might do to others. I just never really wanted to hurt anyone.

When I put the pads on for the first time, my coach, John Federici, started off the practice with a tackling drill. I didn't know much about technique, but I liked his tackling philosophy. My coach said, "When you go after a ball carrier, hit him hard and with everything you have. Good tackling is projecting yourself through a target. This way, you are hitting and the offensive man is getting hit. Now a couple of you jump in here and try it."

Some of the guys were making pretty good tackles and some of them weren't. When my turn came to make a tackle, everyone quieted down. Coach Federici had never seen me tackle before and he sort of wondered what was about to happen. Then in a split second of clashing pads and painful screams, Coach Federici understood the silence before my first tackle. Actually, it was no big deal, even though I did knock the ball carrier out. Everyone who knew me expected a knockout because of the type of drill the coach had set up. One man ran the ball straight at another man, who would attempt to make the tackle. This drill was for men only because it was straight-ahead football. It simply amounted to building up your speed and smashing the ball carrier. For the most part, the running back is usually a little apprehensive about head-on tackles and he tends to back off. Any man that has the courage to really drive his body through the target while making the tackle is going to hurt the other person. Needless to say, Coach Federici never let me participate in that particular drill again. I think his decision made a lot of guys on our football team very happy.

My early practice sessions were unusual. Everyone else was permitted to go full speed while I was restrained from tackling. The coach said he didn't have enough bodies on the team to risk injuries to anyone (we only had twenty-four players). He said, "Jack, you take it easy. Just play touch football with the ball carrier because I don't want you hurting yourself."

"Coach," I said in reply, "I'm not scared of getting hurt. In fact, it doesn't hurt to tackle people and I really like to hit."

The coach sort of smiled in a peculiar way and said with a big grin, "I know, Jack. I know."

The business about not being allowed to make tackles started to bore me so I asked if I could try some offense. The coach consented, and once again, at least for a couple plays, I was the terror of the gridiron. At first I was used as a running back. I figured if making tackles by driving through a target was effective, then running with the same driving force would work, too. I therefore went out of my way trying to run people over. My theory worked, and I became a one-man wrecking crew. At the time I never realized why I was so effective as both tackler and runner, but I later learned it was just a matter of the proper use of speed. Since I was the fastest man on the team, speed became my advantage. Tackling is mass times velocity. As I said before, the faster and more violently I can drive my body into a target, the more effective my hit will be. In high school I had the ability to start out with quick, strong bursts. I was able to achieve full speed in two steps, and regardless of whether I was running the ball or tackling the ball carrier, I always became the driving force. I was always able to do the hitting instead of getting hit. That was my idea of defensive football.

Still, there was a limit to my aggressiveness. I was aware that tackling and even running the ball required a full-speed style if the end results were to be effective, but I had mixed emotions about actually hurting people. I know it might sound strange, but after I would bust into someone and knock that man cold, it sort of hurt me emotionally. And yet when I seemed to slack off a little, someone would simply run me over, and that hurt even more. Unfortunately, there seemed to be no happy medium in my style of play. After making several flat-footed, half-hearted approaches at tackling and finding myself getting bulled over, I became Mr. Devastation. I was a brutal tackler, but the first lessons I learned were the structures of the rules.

Ghetto football is tougher than a high school football game. Playing around the various towns in New Jersey, you had to be tough or you could get killed. The guys, I guess because of their backgrounds, seemed to be nastier and would take cheap shots. Sometimes one or two guys would try to hold you up while another would try to tear your head off with a high tackle. There was an old saying that you were supposed to step on legs that were sticking out of a different colored uniform. Also, if you didn't get blood on your jersey, someone else's blood, then you weren't doing your job. I wasn't scared to play the game hard, but in my estimation there was a difference between rough football and insanity.

I had a lot of respect for my high school coach. Our coach taught sportsmanship, and it made me proud to play for that type of person, when many other coaches actually encouraged cheap-shot animalism. As a sophomore and a junior, I received some minor bumps because of cheap shots. It wasn't uncommon for another team to pile on, or you could be tackled five yards out of bounds, or you could get hit ten seconds after the whistle. Dirty play was more dominant in the games against the wealthier schools or better areas we went into. For some reason, many of these schools seemed to resent a team made up of mostly blacks and boys that came from the ghetto, and the officiating also reflected the prejudiced attitude. One time we ran over one team and scored touchdown after touchdown. But every scoring play we had was called back for one infraction or another. We were called dirty names, and played the game without the aid of a fair judge. During this game I began to hate the other players, but it still never entered my mind to play dirty against the other team. I played hard and made several violent tackles, but I just couldn't bring myself to hit a man who was out of bounds or to make a hit after the whistle. I guess my attitude was a reflection of the coaching I was receiving and the influence of my parents. I know it wasn't much fun getting hit late but I can honestly say that I never went out and tried to take a cheap shot. It hurt me to see one of our guys get injured because of a late hit, but even in high school I tried to keep my aggression channeled within the structure of the rules. Sometimes, I admit, I did things differently, but nonetheless I was always a fair player.

I remember playing a scrimmage with an all-white team. We were taking a terrible physical beating. It wasn't because the team was good or hard-hitting, it was because of their expertise in late hits, clipping, biting, and kicking. Even though the other team was cheating and doing everything rotten, we were still running up the scores. All during the game one of their defensive backs was taking cheap shots and hitting late. He really got on my nerves. In all the football games I have ever played, this was one guy I wanted to really get, but as it was, he seemed to avoid the real action and was busy looking for our people when their backs were turned. Well, on one play, I broke out around the end with the ball and had about seventy yards of green grass between myself and the goal line. Just as I was ready to turn on the burners, I saw him coming after me. Actually, he had no chance of catching me and he knew it, but he was making it look good. He was pumping his arms and legs and running like some fool trying to cut me off. Somewhere between six points and the forty yard line, I got this inspiration to cut back and run the dirty player over. I slowed down a little and gave him the proper angle on me. When he was about five yards from me, I cut back against the grain, put my head down, and buried the man. That was the only time in my career that I can honestly remember trying to hurt a man. Other times, I tackled hard and violently, but it wasn't for the purpose of injuring my opponent.

During my junior year I started thinking that maybe I had a future in football. Already I was an All-State player and had even made the high school All-American team. But between the ghetto and professional football was college. It was easy to see that if I didn't work hard in school and pay the price with athletics, my future was going to be bleak. I've seen how the ghetto can reach up and grab you by the throat, but then again, all the losers I knew actually wanted to lose. Sure, it was a tough life style and there isn't anything pretty about garbage rotting in the streets and ten people living together in a three-room apartment. But just about everyone in the ghetto stays there because they want to spend their days feeling sorry for themselves instead of working their way out. My parents were poor and we had it tough, but my father went to work every day and was trying to improve. I know there were times when he looked around at his world and how his children were living and it hurt, but he realized, too, that it was only going to be temporary. To me, my father was a king because he believed in better days to come and went out and worked toward this goal and my mother was a queen because she kept our clothes clean, the house in good order, and taught us children about the Good Lord and the better things that life had to offer. I knew that in spite of my environment I could get out, but I would have to work and work. It probably would have been easier to give into the screams of the ghetto, start running in the streets with the gangs, and take trips on drugs, but my highs came from football and doing well in school. Even though I grew up in the ghetto, I always believed that I was the luckiest guy in the world. Someday I was going to work my way from the hell of this broken cluttered world out into that area where the sun would shine a little brighter. I wasn't going to let the ghetto own my soul.

When my senior year came along, I had developed into one of the top high school players in the country. I was 5 feet 11 and weighed 205 pounds. Physically, I had reached full maturity, in fact, I still carry the same weight. There were people who said I looked out into the world from narrow slits in a hardened face. They said I was mean and nasty and had no regard for my personal safety or the safety of others around me. But they mistook grim determination for meanness; I was only a young man with a mission in life. I wanted out of the ghetto; and football and education were my road toward success. Because of my purpose, I dedicated myself to helping my parents, my brothers and sisters, and of course, me, from the dirt and filth of the ghetto. Every day was another day closer to the time when we could leave, and I never gave up. It was hard work in the classroom and on the practice field. But then, one day, my high school career had ended and college scouts and recruiters came from all over the country to talk with me about the future. Finally, after three years of hard work on the football field and solid grades in the classroom, I was taking my first step out of the ghetto and into a better world.

4

RECRUITING WARS

I have often been asked which phase of football in my career has been the most demanding. Some people think it is trying to cover a quick receiver, while others might consider it trying to bring down a big running back. The truth of the matter is that the real strain of my career has never come from the physical or mental combat of battle. The most pressure I ever faced during my football career was trying to decide which college I wanted to attend. Part of the pressure came from the fact that I had enough intelligence to realize that college could be the chance to launch a career in the NFL, but more important, it was an opportunity for me to receive an education. Football is a fine and wonderful game, but between high school and professional football were many ifs. I wasn't about to put my future on thin ice. I wanted my future to be on solid ground, and education was my primary reason for college. Football was important, but not as important to me as preparing myself for a career in a good, paying profession.

I guess letters started piling up in my coach's office during my junior year in high school. Although it was flattering to think colleges were interested enough to start writing to me when I was only a junior, Coach Federici felt it wasn't the time for me to even begin to consider which college I wanted to attend. My coach simply filed all the letters in a big box with the promise I could start reading them after my football career at Passaic High School was over.

Several times during my junior year a coach or scout

from one of several universities broke through my coach's defense and actually approached me. But whenever Coach Federici got wind of what was going on, he he quickly took a broom to anyone near me. In a way it was good, because one year of maturing means a lot to a high school kid. I know that in one year many of my values changed, and by the time I was a senior, I had my priorities in proper order—education first, then football. As a junior I had been thinking about All-Pro status in the NFL without even considering four years of college football as the necessary stepping stone between high school and professional football.

When Coach Federici finally opened the door and let the recruiters in, my headaches only just began. At first I felt it was going to be quite simple. I wanted my parents to see my college games so I picked Syracuse. It was a major college, had a good academic program, and had produced some of the great running backs in the game. Jim Brown, Floyd Little, and the late Ernie Davis had all starred for the Orangemen and gone on to professional fame. I liked the idea of following in their footsteps.

When I started talking to coaches and recruiters from the different colleges around the country, it suddenly became quite frustrating and confusing. One school in the South, a white school, wanted a token black. That was during the height of the equality bunk that was spreading across the country and the recruiter from that school said, "If we have to start putting blacks into uniforms, we may as well go after the best talent in the country." I didn't know whether to consider myself flattered or to smack the man in the mouth. I mentioned the incident to my coach, and he had that school barred from talking to any of the athletes on the Passaic team.

Then there was the all-black school and its recruiter, who felt black athletes were better than white athletes. He was in the process of building a National Championship team from colored stars across the country. His remark was something like, "We'll teach them hunky bastards about football!" That was another recruiter who eventually was barred from Passaic.

Still, I kept my head squarely on my shoulders and

made my first visit to Syracuse. It was a delightful week-end. I received something like $300 in cash for expenses, a car to drive around, and even a girl. And the girl was something else! She explained what Syracuse had to offer differently than the coaches did, and to be quite honest, I liked her reasoning. I had almost definitely decided that I would make Syracuse my university for the next four years and that young lady certainly figured into my plans. What made the Syracuse offer even more enticing was the fact that they were going to let me wear number 44. Anyone who knows anything about Syracuse and number 44 knows that all the great running backs in the history of the school wore that number. For many reasons at that time, number 44 meant something to me. It was like being able to follow in Jim Brown's footsteps or maybe even indicated confidence that I would eventually play in the NFL. Whatever, it was special to me, and the memory of my new lady friend and knowledge of that famous jersey number had me thinking Orange and Syracuse.

When I arrived back in Passaic, I told Coach Federici everything that had happened. He was a little disappointed when I told him how I was lured in by the young lady but I assured my coach that even without her, Syracuse was still a very attractive school. He suggested that I think about everything and in the meantime I should get out and see some of the other schools. He said, "After all, they pick up the expenses and I think it's good for you to see what some of the other universities have to offer. That way, you can compare the differences." It was good advice and I took it.

My next stop was Michigan State and a rather rude awakening. At Michigan State I met a young running back from Thomas Jefferson High School in Brooklyn, John Brockington. John and I had the same type of career, All-Everything in high school, and even had the same recruiters after us. We got to rapping about the differences between the various schools, and I started picking up some information. John had been out visiting quite a number of schools and, compared to me, seemed to be an expert. Then he started talking about his trip to Syracuse and a certain young lady. I listened and by the time he finished talking, I could have sworn that he was listening in on my date with my lady. She said the same things to him that she had said to me. They even did the same things that she and I did! What's more, John said, "They'll even give me number 44 if I go there."

Well, it hurt for a little while, but I really didn't have that much time for pain because Michigan State had provided me with another young lady who had a way of making me fall in love with the Spartans. But now I was starting to seriously consider what my coach had said about looking around before I decided at which university I planned to spend the next four years of my life.

I came away from my MSU trip believing that all schools would tell a young athlete anything to get him signed up. It seemed like bending the rules or outright lies and made me extremely cautious. If a school was willing to bend the rules to get me there on a four-year athletic scholarship, then maybe they would also break the rules to get rid of me should I fail to measure up to expectations. It became a serious concern of mine.

After several more trips I had something like $700 in cash left over, five new young ladies who were madly in love with me, the promise of high-paying off-season jobs, and any type of car I wanted. I got to the point where I really enjoyed visiting a university and found little ways of getting more money from them. It all became a big game and the cash kept flowing in. One school gave me a job in Passaic working at a drugstore—one of their alumni members owned the store and they really wanted me. Another school promised me $200 a week under the table, a better paying job for my father, and something special for my mother. I never found out what they meant by something special for my mother, but they hinted about new furniture. It was becoming unbelievable, and then came my trip to Notre Dame. I figured that if the other schools were making all these wild promises, then Notre Dame was really going to offer a fantastic deal.

I arrived in South Bend on a rather cold and snowy day. That sort of put the damper on everything, because I hate cold weather. They took me over to meet Coach Ara Parsegian. Thus far no one had made any special promises, so I naturally figured Ara would make the full presentation.

Sitting in his office, I noticed there were several other players waiting to go in to see him, and I really didn't like the idea of wasting time. I waited for a half hour and noticed that he was taking exactly fifteen minutes per player. That was strange. Then my turn came. To be honest, when I walked into his office, I didn't know if I should kiss his ring or shake his hand. Everything seemed so pious and upright, and then there were all these priests scattered here and there throughout the campus. Well, it made me feel like I was in a big church or even in the Vatican City and Ara was His Holiness.

Ara was calm and cool as he rattled off his Notre Dame pep talk. I could see there was little or no sentiment attached to the deal and he offered nothing special. The meeting was quite matter-of-fact, and when my fifteen minutes had expired, so had the meeting.

The next stop was the gym. The assistant coach had me fitted with gym clothes and tennis shoes. For what, I didn't know, but then we went out on the main floor. The coach said, "Jump up and touch the rim."

"What?" I asked.

"Jump up and touch the rim. I want to see how high you can jump."

I wasn't interested in basketball and I wasn't interested in jumping in the air. When I stopped for a few seconds to think about the situation, I realized I wasn't interested in Notre Dame, either. I didn't jump up and attempt to touch the rim.

When I started out, selecting a college seemed a very easy decision, but now, after having made many trips to the different schools, it was becoming a mind-boggling experience. I didn't know what school I liked. The pressure was getting to be overwhelming. I almost got to a point where I was ready to say the hell with it all and go work on the garbage truck. Every time I turned around, there was a coach or scout knocking at the front door with a thousand reasons why I should attend his university. It all began to sound like a big recording; a different face, a different voice, but the same old story. I needed a change of pace. I needed something different that would help me decide, and I didn't know what the answer was going to be.

During the early spring Joe Paterno from Penn State called me, and he was different. Joe explained that Penn State was a highly accredited learning institution with an excellent football program. Joe slanted his talk toward the educational aspects of my career, with football as his number two concern. He was a down-to-earth type of guy, and we talked about making plans for a trip to Penn State. Just talking with the man on the phone had me excited, and I started thinking that maybe Penn State was the answer to my situation. Joe never promised any girl or money under the table, and nothing was mentioned about wearing any special jersey. I liked the way Paterno presented himself and the university.

Then, about a week after the Paterno call, I was playing basketball with several of the guys when a young dude came up to me and said, "Hey, Tate, I think a sweeper salesman just went up to your house and your mother let him in."

There had been this slicker going around the neighborhood trying to get people signed up for sweepers. It was one of those $10 down and $5 a month for the next fifty years deals. It was also rumored that the sweeper salesman was a con artist who ripped people off for the $10 down and never delivered the sweeper. If it was that sweeper salesman talking to my mother, then I was going home and do some talking to him. My mother has one of those hearts that won't say no. I don't care what the deal is, she'll buy it; and I just didn't like the idea of a slicker trying to con her.

I dropped the ball and took off over fences and up through the alleys. Half the guys in the neighborhood took off after me. Everyone thought that if I caught up with the dude, there would be trouble, and they all wanted to watch the action. Actually, I really didn't have any plans to get physical with the dude unless he started giving me some lip, but still, I was going to let him know that the suckers don't live on this side of town.

I banged open the front door and heard my mother say, "There's John David now." I walked into the kitchen real cool, but I stopped in my tracks when I saw Woody Hayes. Hell, he wasn't a sweeper salesman.

My mother said, "J.D., this is the nicest man I have ever met. He's Coach Woody Hayes. My, what a prince this man is!"

I leaned over the back of the chair where my mother was sitting and simply said, "Hi." After all, I had met nearly every coach in the country, so Woody Hayes wasn't anything special to me.

But then Woody quickly let me know I wasn't anything special either when he said, "Hi," and went back to talking with my mother. "Mrs. Tatum, that was the best piece of pie I have ever tasted. You'll just have to give the recipe to my wife."

"Why! Coach Hayes, you say the nicest things. That's our favorite pie. It's banana cream and I make this special crust. . . ."

My mother went on to explain her secret recipe, and Woody stuffed his mouth with another piece of pie and listened. I got the feeling he had come in from Columbus to visit my mother, and the way she was talking to him made it seem like they were lifelong friends. After five or ten minutes, I couldn't see any sense in my leaning on the back of my mother's chair and listening to their conversation. They didn't need me in the room, so I left. To my surprise, no one missed me.

After Woody and my mother talked for about an hour, I went back into the kitchen. The pie was completely gone and Woody was sitting there picking at the crumbs and telling my mother about General Patton and World War II. Then my mother started telling Woody about her father's claims of fighting in the Civil War. It was amazing. Once again, I felt very much out of place.

Several hours later, Woody left. He said good-bye and told me he would see me soon, but that was it. I was shocked. Woody Hayes couldn't have come all the way to Passaic to recruit my mother, and yet he never got around to talking with me. I just couldn't figure it out. I half expected him to lay some money on me or at least give me some pep talk about the Buckeyes and the Rose Bowl, but there was nothing.

After supper I began to realize what actually had happened. My mother said, "You know, John David, I think it would be nice if you went to Columbus and paid Coach Hayes a visit. I think it is a wonderful school and he's so kind."

It wasn't long afterward that I arrived in Columbus to see what Woody Hayes was all about. But I went there maintaining the attitude that Jack Tatum was something special. After all, almost every school in the country had put in a bid for my talents, and some of them were willing to pay a big dollar to get me. I couldn't help but think that Ohio State would make the best offer of all. When you think about hard-nosed football and a winning tradition, Ohio State ranks up at the top. They always seemed to get their share of great athletes, so there had to be some payola involved. I wanted to see the color of Woody's money, even though I still entertained thoughts of visiting Penn State.

It was a surprise when Woody started out by saying, "I don't know what the hell the other schools promised you but I'll make only two promises . . . and I'll keep both of them. When you come here, expect to study. No one gets any grades handed to them. That way, you'll leave a better man than when you came. That's my first promise—to make you a better man. And secondly, I'll make you a better football player. I'm not promising that you'll go off and play in the NFL; I'm only saying that you'll be a better football player. In fact, there isn't a school in the country that will give you a better education in the classroom and better training on the football field. It's just that simple."

I was amazed at Woody's presentation. He was overpoweringly blunt and to the point. There was no mention of money under the table, no young lady to entertain me, no fancy car, no sugar daddy; just education and football. I started talking with some of the other players who had actually spent time under Woody.

Everyone said the same thing: "He's a monster." I couldn't understand. If the man was such a monster, then why did all these players stick it out?

So I asked the obvious question, "If that's so, then why stick?"

Everyone looked at me like I was some kind of a fool. Then one guy stood up and said, "We stick 'cause Coach Hayes is a great man. He doesn't lie, doesn't cheat, and he wants to win."

I couldn't figure out the difference between my conception of a "monster" and how the term was supposed to be applied to the character of Woody Hayes, but there was obviously some difference. Everyone said he was a bastard, but everyone said he was a great guy, too. It was strange but intriguing.

When I went back home, my mother was the first to ask what I thought about Woody, and all I could say was, "Different."

After a few phone calls and my parents' visit to the school, my mother made up her mind; I was most definitely going to OSU.

Recruiting to me was, and always has been, a war. I realize that the NCAA has changed many rules and has really tried to clamp down on any illegal activity, but still, all the high school stars getting ready to consider a college have my sympathy. Selecting a university to attend on a full athletic scholarship is an exhausting experience. I don't think that any kid in the world is actually ready for that type of pressure, but it happens every year. After the high school football season, every university in the United States fires up their recruiting machine and begins digging up the talent.

I know that Ohio State considers their methods the best, and Alabama thinks their way is the best; along with Notre Dame, Purdue, Arizona, UCLA, and even Slippery Rock. Every school has a technique for recruiting high school athletes, but it all comes down to basically the same idea: Get the athelete to sign a letter of intent.

In the state of Ohio there are more than 40,000 high school boys participating in football. When you consider that more than 750 high schools have a football program in the state and that only about 100 of the school boys are considered blue chippers, finding that talent can become a tremendous job. I have only mentioned the state of Ohio, and OSU football covers more than just the Buckeye State. Let's consider that on an average year, Ohio State's scouting system gets into several thousand schools across the country, and that is probably an underestimation. But using that figure, it means that Ohio State scouts actually look at over 100,000 kids across the country. And from the number it will come down to getting serious about only two or three hundred of the best athletes.

The recruiting process all starts with the committeemen. These are the people who have graduated from Ohio State and go into their particular walk of life without forgetting the scarlet and gray. They are always trying to make a contribution to their beloved university. A good example of what I'm talking about occurred in the sleepy little town of Brookfield in northeastern Ohio. Brookfield High School has a total enrollment of possibly five hundred students in the top three grades but they have something very special; a State Championship football team. Winning state championships usually means talent, and Brookfield is loaded. But long before Brookfield won statewide honors, college committeemen, coaches, and scouts flocked to this small town and began verbally attacking the young players. I don't mean it in a bad way, but still, it becomes a verbal attack when every one of the scouts and coaches have their own special talk about the school they represent. After a while the kids start ducking every time someone mentions their name. Hell, when I was in school, I wanted to go out and play some basketball or run around with my lady friends. At first I really wasn't interested in some scout or coach taking up my time. Being a teenager can be a wonderful time of any man's life, and I believe the pressure these young kids receive from big-time colleges is a little ridiculous. At Brookfield they had three blue chippers, Marc Marek, Darwin Ulmer, and John Lott. An average day for these kids consisted of six hours of classroom studies and twelve hours of bullshit from college scouts and coaches.

Committeemen called me from Ohio State and asked me to talk with these young fellows from Brookfield, but I didn't believe in that type of interference. I have met the coach at Brookfield, John Delserone, and his prize athletes, but I won't interfere in anyone's life. I told the coach and his boys, "Ohio State is a nice place. It suited me but you go and look for yourself. Make up your own mind and don't let anyone sway you into a bad decision." But it's tough for these young men to always make the right decision. I know that a lot of universities actually do care about the young people they approach, and I firmly believe Ohio State is one of these schools, but day after day, hour after hour, it becomes a real headache for any young man to try to make the right decision.

I had received over three hundred letters from different colleges and universities. I never realized that there were so many different universities in the country, but they all knew about me. When my coach opened the door and let the scouts in, it became a serious problem. I said before that I was so overwhelmed that I almost threw in the towel, and I wasn't kidding.

I honestly believe that a new system of recruiting should be developed. A high school coach should grade his talent and then, for the blue chippers, let them pick out six major schools and three division II schools to visit. It should be the athlete's selection, and not some coach or scout who starts the meeting. This way, the coach writes to possibly Ohio State and five other schools and tells them about his number one running back. If any of these schools are interested in the young man, then arrangements are made for a visit. The young athlete would be able to visit several schools, get a pretty good overall picture of the situation, and then start making up his mind. If he feels that he would like to look into another university, then his high school coach would make the contact. I believe these young athletes are still kids, even though some of their bodies would argue that point. Still, we should treat this matter with some intelligence, and, most important, give the kids a little consideraton and some room to breathe. If someone doesn't begin to change the rules on recruiting in favor of the young athlete, then I can see people actually getting beaten up and shot at over the whole issue. The pressure to win at any level of college football is overcoming our ability to reason. With hundreds of schools participating in the annual chase for the high school talent, it's going to come down to a matter of broken bones for the recruiters and nervous breakdowns for the kids. Think about it: Every major school has its committeemen, and even Brookfield, Ohio, has its Penn State grads, Ohio State grads, Pitt grads, Maryland, Michigan, Bowling Green, etc., grads. Well, I think you see what I mean. All I can say is that I really thank God for guiding me in the right direction and into the correct decision.

If I were to give any young athlete advice on how to select a school, I think it would first start with honesty. How honest is the recruiter? If the recruiter is filling your head with wild promises, then be wary, because the more promises a person makes, the more difficult it becomes to keep those promises. The next thing to consider is your education. The likelihood of a professional football career is a distant and improbable dream for most athletes, but educating yourself for a workable career is a strong probablity for anyone who has the persistence to work at it. Therefore, education is more important than any football program. But still, there are many quality schools that offer excellent academic programs and still compete on a major level in collegiate football. Ohio State is just one of those schools, and I guess I was just one of those lucky guys who spent four years educating himself and developing into a football player. I knew that if something happened, an injury or whatever, and I wasn't able to participate in sports, I would still have the education to fall back on. Like I said, I was lucky.

5

DIFFERENT STROKES
FOR DIFFERENT FOLKS

Woody Hayes was the head football coach at Ohio State for twenty-eight years. But he's much more. Ask anyone. Just mention his name on the street and the reaction is everything from "prince" to "prick."

My father always calls Woody "Coach Hayes" and my mother referred to him as the "royal prince." She only made that statement once, but Woody is my parents' main man. They trust him and believe in him.

Other folks around the country have different opinions of Woody. Once I heard a little guy say to his friend, "I'm gonna get me the autograph of Mr. Nasty."

He went up to Woody and asked him to sign the program he was holding. Woody did. Then he looked Woody right in the eye and asked, "Are you really nasty all the time?"

Woody sort of smiled and said, "No, just most of the time."

Another time, when I was out for dinner with a lady friend, we got on the subject of strange people we knew. Right away I blurted out, "Woody Hayes!"

The lady sat up and said, "Oh yes, Woody Hayes. He's the governor of Ohio."

Just about everyone from coast to coast knows the name Woody Hayes but most people have never met the man or taken the time to find out about him. The fact is, Woody Hayes is just about everything he has ever been called, but you have to know the man to understand his story. The whole story isn't something you see on TV or read about on the sports page.

Until now the only public statement I have ever made concerning Woody was: "Woody is different. You've got to know the man to understand the man."

Woody Hayes is a man of personality and character, and he can change quicker than the snap of a finger. I've seen Woody travel from his Sunday-morning, go-to-church best to the other side of normal in the time it took him to sucker-punch someone for not paying attention.

At half-time during one game against Northwestern, Woody was talking to the offensive unit about its poor showing. The score was only 21-0, and Woody felt we should have scored at least 40 points that first half. He was upset but he was cool as he paced the locker room pointing out mistakes.

Then my roommate, Phil Strickland, stood up to fix his shoulder pad straps. Phil, an offensive guard, should have been paying attention, because he had made plenty of mistakes, often pulling the wrong way and running over our quarterback. But then, Phil also comes under the heading of strange people I know.

Phil was standing up playing around with his straps when Woody moseyed over toward him. The tone of Woody's voice never changed. When he stood about an arm's length from Strick, the old man lashed out with four or five quick jabs to Phil's head. Then Woody went on talking as if nothing had happened, but Phil had been knocked over backward from the punches to his head. The rest of us helped him get his seat, and to this day I believe Phil still wonders what happened. So do I.

That was just a common type of coaching sucker-punch. It wasn't serious. A lot of coaches use a sucker-punch, or even a solid kick in the can, as an attention-grabber. However, every once in a while Woody will stray from the ranks of normality, and you don't have to play football at Ohio State to see the old man throw a fit. Woody's all-time best performances have come before live TV audiences during the heat of battle. There's just something about a TV game that brings out the worst in Woody. Most coaches dress up for the TV game and say cool things in front of the cameras. Not Woody. He always wears the same old black pants, wrinkled white shirt, 1939 Sears & Roebuck skinny necktie, and baseball cap. If Woody thinks the situation calls for a cuss word, he will cuss. Or if he thinks heavier action is needed, Woody will do everything from chase the officials to kick the fans or even beat up on a cameraman and his camera.

I'm an Ohio State fan and I watch OSU football on TV because I like the action. Don't get the idea I'm praising the *football* action, because that's not the action I'm talking about. I watch Ohio State football because of Woody Hayes. The old man is unpredictable, and it's exciting trying to figure out what he's going to do next.

Several years ago the team went up north for a game with Michigan. It was tough going throughout the game, but Woody was keeping himself under control. He was doing normal things like cussing, stomping up and down on the sidelines, and throwing his clipboard. Then came a five yard penalty, and Woody went off like a big cannon.

I could see Woody's old heart start pumping the blood and the heat coming off his back hit the cold air and turn to steam. The old man was boiling in a few seconds, and everyone around him knew it. When his face turned three shades of red, the other coaches jumped him. It was a funny scene, Woody dragging the coaches across the field swinging and cussing up a storm in the direction of the man who threw the flag.

I believe that if several players hadn't jumped in and helped out, Woody would have dragged the coaches back to Ohio chasing after the official. Finally, the coaches and players got the old man down and wrestled him back to the sidelines. Everything seemed under control, but Woody got to his feet just in time to see the official stepping off the last few yards of another penalty against Ohio State. Lip readers from coast to coast saw Woody ask, "What the hell was that all about?"

An unthinking young freshman player informed Woody, "Coach Hayes, the dude laid the flag on you for coming after him."

Woody let the statement register for a second and then he went berserk, screaming and cussing. He threw his baseball cap at the ground and ran along the sidelines shaking his fist at the official and cussing him out. The official wasn't listening and paid no attention to Woody's verbal assault. I felt Woody was going to sucker-punch the official or at least give him a kick in the tail but he fooled me. This was a big TV game, and Woody had one better up his sleeve.

The old man ran over to the yardage markers, grabbed them up like a bundle of sticks, and threw them onto the playing field. That got everyone's attention, including the man with the yellow flag. It was fifteen more yards against Ohio State.

In a final fit of defiant rage, Woody stormed onto the field and started jumping up and down on the yardage markers. This time the other coaches and players let him alone. Everyone was so amazed or shocked at Woody's action that they decided it would be safer to stand back and let the old man burn himself out beating up on some metal poles.

That was a dark day in the career of Wayne Woodrow Hayes. Woody lost all the arguments with the officials; he lost the game; and, most likely, he gave up any claim to the good fellowship award for the best-behaved college coach.

Most of Woody's career has been sunshine and roses, but there have been a few other dark spots worth mentioning. I'd say that November 19, 1977, might be one date in history that Woody scratched out with a black crayon. That was the day he took the team up to Ann Arbor for the big game with Michigan.

To appreciate exactly what did happen on that day, a person must understand the rivalry between Ohio State and Michigan. Part of the football season's bitterness between the two schools comes from the fact that for about the last ten years this game has decided the Big Ten Championship and who goes west to the Rose Bowl. Championships and Rose Bowls are a very important part of Big Ten football, but the real story is hidden behind closed doors, where two opposing coaches spend most of their free time throwing poison darts at

each other's photograph. Of course, I'm talking about
Woody Hayes and Bo Schembechler.

Bo Schembechler is the head coach at Michigan, but
his career actually started at Ohio State. As head coach
material there, he planned to sit back and wait for
Woody to retire. It was a good plan and packed merit,
but Woody had his retirement scheduled for sometime
during the next century. When Bo realized that Woody
might have a lifetime contract with OSU, his next plan
was to blend his coaching philosophy into the old
man's system.

Even though Schembechler was blessed with talent
and had a future in coaching, Woody wasn't interested.
Ohio State might have six practice fields, one dozen
trainers, and 85,000 seats in the stadium, but there is
only one head coach in Columbus. If Bo suggested a
running play around the left end, Woody sent the offense to the right. If Bo got on the elevator and said
"Up," Woody pressed the down button. It came to a
point where if Bo had said there wasn't any Santa Claus,
Woody would have insisted he believed in one.

At first, tones were quiet, but as their personalities
clashed daily, everyone knew something was bound to
happen . . . something serious. Before long Bo and
Woody started spitting and punching at each other. One
day at a meeting, Woody became so riled up over a few
remarks Bo had made (not personal remarks, just coaching judgments) that Woody ended the meeting by
throwing a metal chair at Schembechler.

Assistant Coach Schembechler was a pain in the
neck for Woody Hayes, but Head Coach Bo Schembechler of Michigan moved that pain to a lower area of
the old man's anatomy. It was one thing for Bo Schembechler to run all over the country recruiting high school
stars for Woody; it was quite another story when the old
man would stroll up to a prospect's door only to see
the new head coach of Michigan sitting in the living
room wearing an I-just-stuck-it-to-you smile on his
face. That's when everything suddenly became serious.
No one was permitted to use the word "Michigan" in
Woody's presence. The big football game had just become a war.

I'm sure that Bo and Woody would have preferred to face each other in some alley behind the stadium and settle the issues once and for all, but school policies and NCAA rules frown on coaches punching each other in public. Much to Woody's and Bo's dismay, it's all settled on the football field with the football players.

I still think it would be more exciting to have Bo and Woody stand on the fifty yard line and let them explain their coaching philosophies to each other. That would prove more interesting than any football game. In 1977 ABC Sports must have had the same idea because they placed minicameras on the sidelines to watch the reactions of each coach. It wasn't the same as Woody and Bo trading insults and punches at mid-field, but it added color to an otherwise boring game.

During the season in Big Ten play, Michigan and Ohio State have the horses to beat up on the less talented schools by just blasting running backs up the middle for touchdown after touchdown. But when they play against each other, all their power and talent is neutralized and the game settles into a matter of few yards gained and fewer points scored. With each snap of the ball the offensive team inches forward into a virtually impenetrable defense and the ball carriers stumble over the arms and legs extending from the mountain of twisted bodies. It's a good sedative, but not much of a football game. Still though, the coaches, who soon lose sight of the real objective (to score points and win), keep blasting away at the middle just as though they were standing at center ring slugging it out in the last round.

I was watching this particular game on television, and several friends stopped by to watch with me. Someone asked, "Hey, Tate, I'm startin' to notice a bad look in Woody's eyes. Any chance of him getting serious before the game is over?"

The situation was getting serious. Michigan, blasting and struggling most of the afternoon, had managed a 14–6 lead. Time was running out when Ohio State took over the ball deep in Michigan territory, but they needed a touchdown and a two-point conversion for Woody to go home with a tie.

I answered my friend, "I think Ohio State will screw up and lose the game. When that happens, Woody will punch the cameraman into the ground. I know the old man. He's been frustrated all afternoon and now he's just like a rattlesake. Woody will strike at the first thing that comes near him."

The other coaches and players knew anything could happen and they knew Woody. They moved away. At the end, the only one standing near the old man was the cameraman. He obviously didn't know any better.

I started telling some stories about Mrs. Anne Hayes, Woody's wife, and how serious she was over the Michigan game. One time she wrote a letter to a friend who lives on Michigan Avenue in Chicago and she penciled on the envelope, "Ugh! Can't you change streets?"

Another time, when Woody's oldest son finished high school, Mrs. Hayes said, "Steve, I'll pack your bags and we'll send you to any college in the country except one. If you pick Michigan, I'll throw you out on the sidewalk and your bags after you."

I finished the stories just as Ohio State fumbled the ball and Michigan recovered. Michigan could sit on the ball for the next minute of play and then start making plans for the trip west.

The ABC camera caught Schembechler's reaction, a half-smile and a big sigh of relief. On the other side of the field it was different. When the cameraman zoomed in to get a close shot of Woody's face, I could see that his heart was shattered. The frustrations of the day, and the year, nearly brought him to tears, but only for a second. Then something terrible happened to Woody's face and he became a monster.

In a fit of rage Woody rushed the cameraman, swinging with wild lefts and rights. The cameraman was able to slip the punches but his camera was taking a terrific beating. I saw those big fists banging into the lens followed by distorted pictures of the crowd and sky. Then everything blacked out.

There was no excuse for a coach punching a camera or attacking a cameraman. ABC didn't have anything to do with Ohio State's fumble or Woody's loss but

Woody repeatedly uses questionable tactics. There isn't any explanation that can justify his actions.

Without a doubt that was the darkest day in the tantrum-throwing career of Wayne Woodrow Hayes, but the darkest night was still to come and quite another story.

Nineteen-seventy-eight was a bad year for Woody and the Buckeyes. The season started off with a loss to Penn State, but Woody took everything in stride. He didn't punch any cameramen or cameras and I think he even may have congratulated Joe Paterno, the winning coach. I'm sure Woody's display of sportsmanship surprised a national television audience, but not me. Woody doesn't slug people or things when he honestly believes the best team won. Obviously, Penn State was the better team even in Woody's estimation.

After the Penn State loss, the Bucks won a few games, lost another one, and were tied once. Naturally, Woody wasn't the happiest gentleman in the world but it was still early in the season and there was the Big Ten title to consider. Although OSU had fielded the weakest defensive team in the history of the university, Woody managed to keep the title hopes alive, and once again it came to the November showdown with the team from up north and Coach What's-His-Name.

But for the third time in three years, Coach Schembechler stuck it to Woody and Michigan packed for their annual trip west while the Bucks were scheduled for a December 29 date at the Gator Bowl. Woody didn't kick, punch, or spit at anyone, and in keeping with the spirit, he also didn't congratulate anyone. Deep down inside I'm sure he would have still liked to get that other coach by the neck and settle the Michigan-Ohio State issue once and for all, but the old man just sort of smoldered off the field.

In spite of a regrettable and preferably forgotten season, Woody had the Bucks sky high for that Saturday night tilt with Clemson. After all, bowl games are usually considered the beginning of a new and fresh season and not the conclusion of a disastrous one. At least, that's what Woody believes and who would dare discuss that point with him?

From the opening kick-off, it was readily apparent that OSU was a stronger and more physical team than Clemson. The Buckeyes controlled the ball, had more first downs, more rushing yardage, and more passing yardage. In fact, they led in every department except scoring. Late in the game the out-gunned Clemson Tigers were clinging tenaciously to a slim 17–15 lead but Woody's boys were pounding closer and closer to the goal line.

With two minutes to play, I opened my big mouth and told my friends (the same ones that watched Woody's bout with the camera), "I got a feelin' the Bucks are going to screw up, and look out for Woody when they do!"

Exactly three seconds after those very words fell from my lips, OSU's young quarterback, Art Schlicter, lifted a perfectly thrown spiral into the waiting arms of Charlie Bauman. This was the beginning of a serious problem for OSU because Charlie was the middle guard for Clemson. That particular play sealed the Buckeyes' Gator Bowl defeat and the end of Woody's coaching career.

Actually, Bauman seemed to be one surprised dude when a football miraculously appeared in his arms, but after a split second of standing there looking dumbfounded, Charlie started running toward the Clemson goal line. Near the sidelines, he ran into a host of nasty Buckeyes and Charlie was blasted out of bounds.

What happened next actually surprised me. I've known Woody for many years and in that period of time, I have come to expect the unexpected from Woody. Woody is different and he does different things. Once you get to know Woody, he could show up for practice wearing ice skates in the middle of summer and it wouldn't shock or surprise you because you know that Woody is different. After the interception and collision near the sidelines, I actually expected Woody to punch or kick the hell out of Charlie Bauman. To my dismay, the old man bent down and helped the Clemson lad to his feet. I was shocked. I was amazed at Woody's display of sportsmanship and, quite frankly, I was speechless. It was so uncharacteristic of

Woody, and for a second he really had me going. But then Woody became Woody. After helping Bauman to his feet, Woody sucker-punched him and followed up with two roundhouses from left field. The first one landed on Bauman's face mask, the second got him in the throat, and the third bounced off his shoulder pads. From that point on, it got real nasty. Several of Woody's boys jumped in and tried to break up the scene but Woody turned on them. Normally, when a fight breaks out during a football game, it's one team against the other, but on this night, everyone jumped Woody and the old man held his own.

Keith Jackson and Ara Parsegian were broadcasting the game (they also did the Woody Hayes vs. ABC Camera fight) and they just played dumb. Everyone in the world who watched that game saw Woody Hayes slug Bauman, after watching the instant replay, but Keith and Ara started asking each other "What happened?" What happened was that Woody Hayes lost to an inferior team and Charlie Bauman became the focal point of a season full of pent-up frustrations.

I realized at that moment that Woody was saying good-bye to coaching and Ohio State. He realized it, too, as he walked from the field surrounded by protecting players. Maybe I have made sport of the situation, and in a way it is funny, but in many more ways it is sad. An incident like that is shameful to Ohio State, the Big Ten, and college football, but the one that carries the scar has got to be Woody. Because of that incident and other ones that started back in 1959, Woody Hayes will never be judged on the accomplishments of his football coaching career or his contributions to humanity. Woody Hayes is a great man, and few people will ever realize how great he is.

The next day it was official, and newspapers from coast to coast carried the headline, "Woody Hayes Fired!" Woody claimed he actually resigned just before he was fired, but regardless, the man's coaching career was over. For the rest of his life, Woody Hayes will be a branded man.

It didn't take the press long to get into the thick of Woody's recent tantrum, but to my surprise some of the stories were positive. Once in a while some reporter had the guts to tell the whole truth, but for the most part, I'm sorry to say, Woody Hayes was all but strung up from the nearest tree.

About two months after the Gator Bowl, I was watching a boxing match on ABC with the volume turned all the way down. Howard Cosell was doing the fight and regardless of how exciting the action is, Howard has a way of putting me to sleep. Between rounds Howard interviewed Billy Martin, ex-Yankee manager. For some strange reason Billy Martin has always reminded me of Woody Hayes. I can't figure it out, because they certainly don't look alike. Anyway, I turned the volume up and listened. Cosell asked about 1980 and the Yankee job and Billy answered with a "yes, maybe, I hope so." Then Cosell said, "Well, if you don't get the Yankee job, we'd like to schedule you and Woody Hayes for the heavyweight championship fight."

Billy Martin, being an intellectual and perceptive gentleman, replied, "Oh, I'd never fight with Woody, he's a great man." And Billy Martin was right, but Howard had to get in the last words. He said, "On the subject of Woody Hayes and Billy's remark . . . I respectfully disagree."

Giving the man some credit, I will say that from time to time Cosell does have a genuine contribution to offer society. Though most of the time when I listen to him I get the feeling he thinks that maybe there was more than one perfect being that walked the face of this world and Cosell was the second one. People are entitled to their opinion, but national television isn't the place for anyone to smear Woody. I think everyone must realize that Woody is a human, an emotional human, and there isn't a soul in the world that feels worse about Woody's emotional actions than Woody. The man was wrong when he slugged Charlie Bauman; he was wrong when he punched Mike Friedman's ABC camera; he was wrong when he shredded the yardage markers; and he was wrong when he punched photographers and spit on the fans. But you judge a man by his entire life and not by those emotional incidents when he gives in to pressures, loses control, and strays from socially acceptable behavior.

I realize that Howard Cosell is entitled to his opinion of Woody just like I am entitled to my opinion of Cosell. But rather than take a cheap shot at anyone and base my statements on pure opinion, I'll just pretend that Howard is a fine gentleman. However, on Woody Hayes and the questions surrounding his greatness, let me say this. Until you have suited up and worked as a player under Coach Hayes, you really don't have the right to judge the man or brand the man because of his emotional peaks during the heat of battle. I don't know Howard Cosell very well but I do know Woody Hayes. If I had to go into a battle and I needed someone loyal and courageous to cover my blind side, I know damn well Woody would be my man. I know, too, that God hasn't created a more generous, compassionate, or more understandng man than Woody Hayes. Sure, we all know Woody's bad side, his human side, because it's newsworthy. When a coach punches a reporter or a player, the press and public eagerly gobble it up. But when a man gives his blood and sweat to a cause, very few people will ever come to realize and understand that type of dedication.

In 1959 Woody Hayes slugged his first reporter and it was written in the newspapers from coast to coast. Only a select few know, however, that in 1978 he supported the family of an Ohio high school football coach dying of cancer. Sure, we all know that he shredded the yardage markers during a football game but how many of us know that Woody Hayes sponsored a poor starving Vietnamese family emigrating to the United States of America? It's all too easy for us to throw dirt on the man's name for the seconds of his life when he does wrong but in so doing, must we bury over sixty years of self-sacrifice and accomplishment? I've seen Woody scream at and slap some of his players for not paying attention but I've also seen him hug and brag about the same ones. It's often been said that Woody's players will not say anything bad about Woody. Maybe, just maybe, it's because we know Woody and we actually sometimes understand the man.

When I see Woody go berserk and punch or kick at someone or even something, I don't like those actions. But then, when I consider the total picture of Woody Hayes and what he represents to humanity and college football, I respect him and find myself very proud to have been a small part of his life. Woody is simply a competitor; the kind of man you want playing on your side and not against you. Woody is the type of man that will lead his troops into battle rather than sit back and tell them how to fight. Woody Hayes gives much more than he takes, and in my estimation that is the real test of a man.

I've said it more than once, "Woody is different." He can be softer than pudding or nastier than sin. Woody can read from the Good Book and sound like a hell-fire-come-back-to-Jesus preacher one minute; the next minute he's foaming at the mouth and running around like a beast from the pit. The old man can be shocking or amazing; he can make you cry or he can make you laugh.

I remember getting suited up for practice on one occasion when the weather was horrible. There was lightning, heavy thunder, high winds, and rain. No one gave a serious thought to actually going outdoors and practicing. No one except Woody.

Everyone was milling around the lockers going through the motions of getting ready while Woody stood by the window watching the clouds. Then Woody started waving his arms and screaming, "Hurry up! Hurry up!"

First reactions were, "The old man's been struck by lightning." Then we realized Woody was serious. He wanted us to get ready and go outdoors.

Woody said, "Hurry up and get ready! I'm gonna make it stop."

Instead of laughing in his face (this was Woody after all), we hid our faces inside our lockers and busted up. It was funny. I mean the wind was rocking the building and the rain was coming down so heavily you couldn't see out the window. Then there was the lightning. And Woody was going to make it stop!

We suited up, and Phil Strickland said, "Okay,

Coach, we're ready on our end. How you doing on your end with the weather?"

That did it. Everyone burst out screaming and laughing at Woody. The wind was lifting the building off the foundations, and Strick kept going, "Hey, Coach, I said we're ready. When's the good weather going to be ready?"

Our sides hurt from laughing but then an amazing thing happened. Woody opened the door and said, "Okay, Strickland, lead them out, but hurry up 'cause I don't know how long I can hold it off."

Strick looked outside. The wind and rain had stopped. The gray clouds were still up there swirling around but no wind or rain. Amazing.

Cautiously, we all stepped out of the locker room and followed Woody and Phil over to the practice field. Woody kept saying, "Hurry, hurry, hurry."

We practiced for more than an hour under threatening skies but it didn't rain one drop. After Woody had gone over everything, he said, "Okay, hurry back inside. I can't hold it off any longer."

Everyone looked for Strick to see what smart remark he was going to make, but much to our surprise, he and Woody were making tracks toward the locker room. Just then, lightning smacked near one of the goal posts and we took off running.

As Woody slammed the locker room door shut, it started again. Rain and hailstones the size of golf balls pelted the door, and we heard a loud roaring noise as someone screamed, "Tornado!" Everyone saw a huge whirling cloud dance right up the middle of the practice field and bounce back up into the clouds.

Most of us didn't know what to say, but Phil started praising Woody. Phil said, "Hey, Coach, that was great the way you held back that tornado! Real cool."

Woody sort of acknowledged Phil by tipping his cap as he turned to look out the window.

"Hey, Coach," Phil was shouting again, "you ever walk on water?"

Woody turned to Phil with a strange look and said, "Not recently."

From that day on, Phil Strickland and Woody Hayes

started to hit it off. That was one of the strangest things I had ever seen because Phil didn't get along with anyone.

Strick was my roommate and he was *strange*. Some days he was easygoing; other times he wanted to fight and I never knew why. Anyway, one day I accommodated Phil and we went at it.

The fight started over his bed. Most people will fight over a lady or money or something serious, but not Phil. When he came into the room, I was sleeping on his bed. He jumped me and we started. After a few minutes of slugging it out in the room, we both agreed someone could get hurt. More serious yet, we might ruin the furniture and Woody would get mad. So we walked over to the elevator, went down into the lobby, and walked outside.

Phil was the strangest guy I have ever fought. I'd drive my fist down his throat, pick him up, and throw him in the bushes, and he'd get up and say, "Tatum, you ain't proved nothin' to me. You're gonna have to do that again."

I did it again, and again, and again, but Phil wouldn't quit. Later (it seemed like hours), we were both getting tired, so some of the guys watching broke it up and called it a tie. Two seconds later Phil was my buddy again.

Most of the time Phil was hard to understand. Maybe that's why he and Woody started to get along. It didn't make sense. For example, one time the offense was practicing a new play Woody had designed and the guards kept making mistakes. The old man started cussing and throwing his clipboard. It was a good bet that whoever screwed up next was going to get punched. Woody screamed at the guards, "We've run this play five thousand times and five thousand times we've screwed it up. Is there anyone that can run the damn thing right?"

No one in his right mind would have volunteered, but Phil stuck up his hand and said, "I can run that play, Coach. I'll show 'em how to do it."

Phil sounded so confident that if I didn't know him, I'd have sworn that he was going to run the play right.

But I, just like everyone else, knew Strick, and we all burst out laughing.

"What the hell's so funny?" Woody wanted to know.

"Yeah, what's so funny?" Phil wanted to know.

After Phil ran the play, both he and Woody found out what we had already known would happen. Just as expected, Phil ran the wrong way and trampled the quarterback into the ground.

The old man was mad. Screaming, he quickly turned toward Strick and drew back his fist. At that moment, Woody said, "If it's not you [meaning Strick] screwing up, then it's you [meaning one of the other guards]," and his punch sailed right on past Strick's head and landed on the other guard's jaw.

I figured that because Woody had one member of the team who honestly believed in him, he wasn't going to destroy Phil's dedication with a sucker-punch he could use on another, less dedicated guard. The old man had someone he could depend on, if you want to depend on Strick, and that was Woody's ace in the hole.

During our senior year, Phil Strickland proved beyond a doubt that he and Woody were pals to the end. The rumors started that some school official wanted artificial turf in the stadium, and the team rebelled. Anyone who has played on astro turf doesn't like it. It is a harder surface, and you can feel the game and the hitting in your body for days afterward. Not only that, the artificial surface doesn't give like grass and you can scrape and burn the skin on your knees and elbows.

Woody called a special team meeting and started to explain artificial turf. It was his way of brainwashing everyone into believing that fake turf would make us faster and better. Woody said, "Not only is it a faster modern surface, but think of the advantages during bad weather . . . no more cold, muddy uniforms."

I was sitting next to Strick and he leaned over and whispered to me, "Hey, Tate, why doesn't Woody just make it stop raining on all game days? That's cheaper than gettin' fake grass."

After explaining the "advantages," Woody said, "I've talked long enough. You people have to play the games so it's all up to you. If you want to be modern, then vote for the new turf and you'll get it."

Sixty-six players quickly cast their votes against the turf; only one player was in favor of Woody's "modern look." Afterward, Phil Strickland said, "Damn, Tate, I thought everyone was going to vote for the new grass. Didn't anyone hear what Woody said about making us faster?"

Strick never was noted for his logic, so someone pointed out, "Strick, the other team plays on the same field, too."

Woody had a democratic system at Ohio State, but just like Woody, his system was different. Woody was always the last man to vote. That way he only has to vote one time if there is a tie or as many times as he needs to win his point. At Ohio State all elections are close, but Woody always wins by one point. With Woody's sixty-six votes and Phil's one, Ohio State, by a narrow margin, went modern.

Woody Hayes is a dictator and the most stubborn man I have ever known. He goes rushing off the deep end and slugs photographers and cameras; he kicks fans, sucker-punches players, and hates Michigan. But in spite of Woody's shortcomings, I trust the man and I, like my parents, believe in him. Woody is a human being and he makes mistakes, but he also goes to the extremes when it comes to hard work, fair play, and honesty.

Sometimes I think that if Woody Hayes fell into a river and was drowning, I'd jump in and try to save him. Other times, I'd probably throw him some chains and say, "Grab hold, Coach."

Woody is the type of character that you can't love all the time or hate all the time. He's different.

Actually, the very first time I met Woody, I realized he was different. After all, most college coaches and scouts tried to recruit me, while Woody recruited my mother, and she recruited me. That was just a normal type of different. When I say that Woody is different, I mean much more than just being normally different. It all started when I was just a freshman scrimmaging the varsity team. I came to OSU as a running back, but because Woody was different, I eventually asked to be switched to the defensive unit.

As a freshman, Woody expects you to be passive and let the upperclassmen knock the hell out of you. I guess we had a rebellious class because things just didn't work out the way Woody wanted.

Getting back to my first scrimmage against the varsity, Woody carefully instructed me to take the hand-off from the quarterback and drive straight up the middle. Then he went over to the defensive unit and stacked everyone up on the line. He told them I was going to run the ball up the middle. I like contact, but Woody's idea of straight-ahead football wasn't setting very well with me and my classmates. I did as Woody instructed and took the hand-off, and even went as far as to actually try the middle, but there was just no moving those eleven defensive bodies. So I did the obvious thing and broke outside for thirty yards and a touchdown. Scoring on the varsity really wasn't a big deal, because 1967 was a particularly terrible year for OSU. Everyone scored on the Bucks, even the freshman team. But I guess Woody was interested in building the morale of his varsity team and getting beat by a brassy group of youngsters wasn't going to help that issue. Woody had tried to make the varsity look good against the freshman team, and, quite frankly, that was one of his failures.

Jogging back to the huddle after scoring my touchdown, I heard Woody screaming at me. He said, "Tatum, what the hell did I tell you to do?"

"Run the ball, Coach," I answered.

"Run the ball where?" the old man questioned.

"Up the middle where there wasn't any hole."

Well, Woody didn't like my answer and he explained the difference between up the middle and outside. It wasn't important that I had scored, because Woody had ordered me to run the ball up the middle. Right there, I started thinking about my career at OSU. I came to college to play football and not to commit suicide. Woody's conception of freshman offensive football against varsity defense was silly.

I talked with the defensive coaches and let it be known

that offensive football just wasn't my bag. I explained that playing defensive football had always been my childhood fantasy. I reasoned that Woody's style of offense called for a big, 230-pound "foolback," and my mother didn't raise no fool. After a few fumbles and a few no-gainers up the middle, Woody changed me to defense. That was the biggest mistake Woody ever made while trying to build the morale of the " '67" team. As a running back I was getting hit, but as a linebacker, I was doing the hitting. Obviously, it hurts more to get hit than it does to hit, and before long, Woody's varsity running backs started running for the sidelines, slipping in the backfield, making those little mental errors, and even running the wrong way. Woody screamed and bitched at the varsity and called them everything from cowards to chickens, but at press conferences he talked quite differently and bragged about me to the sportswriters. Woody once said, "We have a freshman that hits so damn hard that our varsity running backs are scared to death of him. Jack Tatum is the hardest hitter I've ever coached or seen play the game of football, and next year people on our schedule will believe my words."

There it is: because Woody was different, I became a formidable defensive player. But that's still not the main reason why I consider Woody different.

I know for a fact that many universities have special bonus programs for star athletes. Of course, I'm talking about cash under the table and many other extras. But at OSU things were naturally different. An athletic scholarship at OSU abides by a strict interpretation of university and NCAA rules. Woody will not deviate from these rules one bit, and there is absolutely no pay-off money. Woody's conformity is an honorable way of being different and a quality of his which I can deeply respect. I believe that if a coach breaks rules in recruiting an athlete, he will in all probability break rules in getting rid of an athlete who gets hurt, doesn't play up to expectations, or cannot blend into the system. At OSU I knew because of Woody's principles that regardless of injury or whatever, my education was assured. Playing for and working with a coach who maintains that degree of honor is worth something, even if it's only peace of mind. I guess this all gets back to what I first said about Woody being everything from a prince to a monster.

As an athlete playing for Woody, you get to almost understand him. The upperclassmen usually school freshmen players about the "do's and dont's" of Woody's philosophy, and by the time your senior year comes around, you come to realize that Woody is basically consistent in his philosophy and emotional responses, though still quite unpredictable in his actions. What I mean is that if Woody is losing to an inferior team, he's going to get mad. That is always a predictable emotional level that you know Woody is going to reach. However, one never knows whether he's simply going to kick, spit, punch, cuss, or do something dramatically different. Woody likes to win, he wants to win, and will not accept any other alternative. Personally, I don't think there is anything wrong with developing a winning attitude, but the emotional level where Woody seems to peak is a point in deep space I have never reached.

Fortunately, most of my career with Woody Hayes was a winning effort. As a sophomore, I, along with sixteen other sophomores, started on offense and defense. A starting team consisting of so many second-year men was unheard of, and to be able to win with youngsters was simply unthinkable. But because Woody Hayes made a tremendous coaching effort to that cause, we won and won.

That particular season, 1968, started off with a win over Southern Methodist University and ended on January 1, 1969, with a victory at the Rose Bowl. Although we were a young, inexperienced team, Woody pulled everything together, and we became the National Champions. Woody never let us know how good we were, and every week it took a greater effort on our part to learn more about Woody Hayes and winning.

After two wins in a row over SMU, 35–14, and Oregon, 21–6, we came to our biggest test of the season, Purdue. During the 1967 season Purdue had laid the wood to the Bucks and walked off the field laughing and pointing to the scoreboard, which read 41–6. Woody hadn't forgotten that score.

When you're young and inexperienced you sometimes believe everything you read in the newspapers. I know that although most of the players were eager to play against Purdue, they still felt that Purdue was practically unbeatable. After all, Purdue was the number one team in the country; they had a great quarterback in Mike Phipps and an All-American running back who was one of the candidates for the Heisman Trophy, Leroy Keyes. It seemed like insurmountable odds for us to overcome. Adding to our feelings of inferiority was the fact that Woody had been quoted in the newspaper as saying, "Leroy Keyes is the best back in the country. No one can cover him one-on-one, and it's doubtful that any team can stop him."

Woody's statement was in the Sunday paper, and at practice on Monday he said, "Jack, we're putting in a special defense to stop Keyes. When he plays outside, you move out and cover him. When he's in the back field, you move in and cover him."

"Coach," I said, "that sounds like you're putting me on Leroy man-for-man."

"Yes, Jack, that's what it sounds like and that's what it is," Woody informed me with a queer smile on his pudgy face.

"But, Coach, I read in the newspaper what you said about no one being able to cover Leroy, and . . ."

Woody interrupted, "Jack, that doesn't apply to you. See, Leroy Keyes will read the newspaper, too. He'll believe what he reads, but the truth of the matter is that I know you can cover him one-on-one."

I wasn't sure Woody knew what he was talking about. Keyes was a tremendous running back and receiver. During a game the previous week, he had personally accounted for nearly four hundred yards, as Purdue blasted Wisconsin. But Woody had said, "Trust me," and I did.

As the week developed, I began to understand Woody's defensive philosophy against Purdue. It was quite simple. When Keyes lined up outside, he was a receiver and they threw the ball to him. When he lined up in the backfield, he was a running back and they gave the ball to him. All I had to do was stop him from gaining any yardage. All week long Woody kept on saying, "You see, Jack, you see how simple it's going to be?"

When Saturday came along, I believed that I could, and, quite frankly, would stop Keyes cold. More important, I knew we could win the game. I think it takes a great coach to completely change a team's attitude during the course of one week's time. When we started practice on Monday most of the players looked as though we were already beaten. But by Saturday it was a different story entirely. Even though Purdue was favored by thirteen points, we were certain that we were going to win the game. It wasn't just thinking that we could win, it was knowing we were going to win. That was the big difference, and when Purdue stepped onto the field, they could sense the difference, too.

When the smoke cleared, I had to give the so-called experts credit, for their thirteen-point spread had been exactly correct, except that we had the thirteen points and Purdue had zero. During the game, I stuck with Keyes, and while I didn't exactly shut him out, I did manage to make things quite difficult for him. At day's end Leroy Keyes had rushed for nineteen yards, caught three passes for forty-six yards, and was all but carried off the field on a stretcher as I pounded and blasted him every chance I had. Now, the newspapers carried another story, and it was about me and the fact that someone could stick with Keyes man-for-man. I felt a certain amount of pride because I had done my job. I knew Woody was thrilled, and that made it seem all the more important to me. I guess that's another indication that Woody is really a great man. When his players can take pride in their accomplishments and not be so blind as to miss noticing the old man's satisfaction with everything . . . well, what I'm trying to say is that the major part of my pride came because Woody was proud of me. Even though the UPI Press voted me the "Lineman of the Week," and AP voted me the "Back of the Week" (no one had ever had that happen before), my true reward still came back to Woody. I remembered he had asked, "Trust me," and because of that I had the faith and we won the game.

An undefeated season, Big Ten Championships, Rose Bowls, and a National Championship are but a small part of my experiences with Woody. Writers can record that particular type of history and still never begin to understand the deep and meaningful relationship between a coach and his players. I guess my experiences at Ohio State were better than those of some of the other players who came after me. During my career, we won with Woody and were also able to share losing games with the same man.

In three years we won many games, the exact number I really don't know. But during that same period of time, I clearly remember we lost twice. I remember the games we lost, I remember the scores; how, when, and where it all happened. I remember because it does hurt a little to lose, but maybe also because as a player I felt that somehow I had failed Woody. Maybe he failed us a little, too, but the end result is still the same—losing isn't much fun and you don't like to remember.

My junior year at OSU was a great example of failure. During the first eight games, we had been rated the number one team in the nation. Offensively, we were averaging slightly over forty-six points a game and defensively our first-string unit was virtually impenetrable. In all, we were awesome, and every team on our schedule was aware of that fact, but then it came down to the final game of the year against Michigan. Because of a Big Ten ruling which prohibited any team in our league from going to the Rose Bowl two consecutive years, regardless of what happened at Ann Arbor, we could not return to California that season. I don't look for cheap excuses, but most of our incentive was taken away from the Michigan game by the Rose Bowl rule. Although Woody was sky high and he wanted to win in the worst way, the players were flat. It was by no means a failure on Woody's part, just the wrong day, the wrong year, and the Buckeyes lost, 24–12. I think about that game because of my performance. I wasn't sharp, and even though I kept telling myself "I think we can win," I honestly didn't care. Afterwards, I didn't want to look at Woody, because I knew that I was a part of his feeling of failure. With Woody everything is built around winning and failure. Either you have won the game or you have failed. On that day we failed. That particular loss was most definitely the fault of the players.

Next season it was different. Once again we had little or no difficulty getting through the regular season and made it with a perfect 9–0 record. For the second time in three years I was going to play in the Rose Bowl, and once again the national championship was on the line. I honestly believe that every player on the team wanted to make that trip west and beat Stanford. For most of us it was the last game we would ever play in a Buckeye uniform, and no one wants to lose their last game. Also, national championships are hard to come by, and all we had to do to be number one was to beat Stanford. It certainly wouldn't take any special coaching philosophies to get us sky high for the Rose Bowl, but a mistake in coaching judgments could take away from what we already had.

Before the Michigan game Woody had promised that if we won, our stay in Southern California would be a very pleasant one. He told us that preparing for a Rose Bowl would take a certain amount of work, but he assured us that we would have plenty of time to relax and enjoy life in the sunshine. Actually, we didn't need that incentive to go out and beat Michigan but Woody wanted to be sure. We won, 20–9, and started packing for Los Angeles.

Somewhere between the pep talk for the Michigan game and the plane trip west, Woody forgot what he said about some R and R in the sunshine of California. It all started about ten minutes after our plane lifted from the snow-covered ground of Columbus. When I saw the trainers taking out their bags and the rolls of tape, I realized that something was wrong. As the plane jetted west, the trainers taped everyone's ankles because Woody felt we needed a practice session on California soil. It couldn't wait until tomorrow; it couldn't even wait until we landed and had something to eat. Woody expected us to step off the plane and go to our headquarters, break out the gear, and practice. That was the beginning of the end. We practiced and practiced and practiced. Even though the game was weeks away, we practiced continually. While the Stanford players were on tours of Beverly Hills, the beaches, and Disneyland, and still found time for light workouts, the Bucks practiced. "You know," Woody would exuberantly shout, "Practice makes perfect!" and from somewhere in the crowd of players you could hear a low mumble, "Eat crap."

Most of us had played for Woody four years; some of the players liked him and some didn't. Still, all of us, without exception, respected Woody as a man of his word. For the first time in our collegiate careers, Woody Hayes had backed down on a promise to us. He was anxious to cap an undefeated season with a Rose Bowl victory, and in his overzealousness, forgot the needs of his players. He felt that the formula for winning was: constant practice plus constant discipline equals victory. Hell, he even made us practice on Christmas Eve. It got to a point where everyone literally quit and Woody started getting serious. He began screaming and bitching at everyone thinking it would help. It didn't.

Sometimes, a coach can make a mistake. We didn't need hours of practice to beat Stanford. All we needed was a little understanding, a little fun, and a little work, but Woody wanted to be sure; he wanted another National Championship.

I don't think that Woody realized it then, and maybe he still doesn't understand, but we actually started losing the Rose Bowl and the National Championship on the plane trip west. Woody didn't have the confidence in us to realize that we wanted to win and he didn't need to take any special training and conditioning methods. When it came time for Woody to trust us with an important part of our lives, he didn't, and the results were a half-hearted effort that fell short of everyone's expectations. We lost the game, and this time our failure was Woody's fault.

I'm trying to say that Woody is only human. He has made mistakes because of his emotions and he has made mistakes when it comes to exercising good judgment in relatively unimportant situations. But then again, no coach is perfect all the time and no athlete plays all games at a 100 percent fever pitch. Coaches, like players, have highs and lows; they win and they fail. But one must look at the whole scope of a man's career before making a final analysis of his performance. Coaching and playing are simply the blending of talents to chart a course of action that will ultimately lead to victory.

It may seem that I've been carried away on the subject of Wayne Woodrow Hayes, but the man has made a tremendous contribution to my life. I owe Woody one, and maybe this is my way of repaying a debt.

In talking with my publisher, I was informed that the style and sequence of this particular chapter was jumpy and confusing. Well, that's actually the way it should be. Woody Hayes is a jumpy confusing guy until you get to know him. My publisher felt I should have ended this chapter with Woody's exit from coaching and my personal testimony to the fact he was a straight-shooter. But I don't want to remember Woody that way, and I don't consider him as being finished. Maybe it's because I know that only a part of the man was a football coach, while the rest was a great human being. Football coaches will retire and fade into the ranks of obscurity, while great men will continue to work and rise to unbelieveable heights of accomplishment. Woody Hayes may never again strike at the ABC camera or spit on the fans, but he will continue to move through life in his strange way, with a genuine compassion for people and a special fondness for his boys.

6

COUNTDOWN TO A SUPER BOWL

An Oakland Raider training camp is hardly a stalag of sweat and torture. Most of our practice sessions are held in a relaxed atmosphere. Some of the guys will take a break and sit down on their helmets and smoke. Others will clown around and have a laugh to ease the pressure. Some people think our system is questionable, but look at the game results. The Raiders win more games than any other team in professional football, and that is a fact.

Paul Zimmerman, a sportswriter for the New York *Post,* spent a day with the Raiders before Super Bowl XI. He walked away from that experience shaking his head and saying, "The Raiders may be the flakiest team in football. If they beat Minnesota in the Super Bowl, it might set reason and sanity back a few centuries."

We did beat Minnesota, but reason and sanity are still in the twentieth century. Zimmerman's feelings were understandable, though. The fact is that when you pull all the different talents and personalities of the Oakland Raiders together and have a training camp, *strange* things can start to happen.

A good example of what I'm talking about concerns our left cornerback, Skip Thomas. The first time I saw Skip play, I knew he was Raider material; he liked to beat people up. Skip considers himself a normal USC graduate with a few different ideas about life. Consider his nickname. Sometimes, Skip likes to be called "Dr. Death." He really isn't a doctor, but Skip had his nickname painted on both doors of his Corvette right under the skull and crossbones.

I don't know if it's bad or good for me, but when Skip came to the Raiders out of college, they made him my roommate. I always seem to end up with special roommates.

Skip won't talk to reporters or let anyone take his picture. He says, "Gettin' your picture taken steals part of your soul." As for reporters, Skip doesn't like people, and of course reporters are people. One time a reporter came up to our room to interview *me*. Skip didn't like the questions I was being asked so he threw the reporter out the door.

"The Doctor" plays football from a different world. His body is on the field doing a job but his mind is off traveling to other planets and solar systems. The night before a game Skip will eat four or five full-course meals, drink a bottle of tequila, smoke two packs of cigarettes, and watch TV for hours after all the channels have signed off. Once, I stayed up and watched TV with Skip, but after ten minutes, I couldn't figure out what was happening. Now I just say, "Skip, I'm going to bed. Lower the TV 'cause I've seen that show before and I need my sleep."

Skip has a fascination for motorcycles and fast cars. When the motorcycle craze was going around, Skip had a dream of jumping the Golden Gate Bridge on a bike. He was going to build a ramp in the parking lot at our summer camp and practice by jumping over a couple of hundred cars. Al Davis put a stop to Skip's dream. I don't think Al was worried that Skip would hurt himself; it's just that the Raiders have a lot of expensive cars and Skip might damage one of the Rolls Royces or Caddies. Football players aren't poor.

Another time, Skip and Clarence Davis, one of our running backs, got into a debate about which was faster, a Corvette or a motorcycle. It was right back to the parking lot. C.D. was gunning the Corvette and Skip was on the bike. Al Davis didn't get there in time to stop the race and when they zoomed across the finish line, there wasn't enough parking lot left to stop the car or bike. C.D. banged off a few parked cars and slid into the practice field while Skip jumped off the bike and landed in a ditch. No one was hurt, but Al Davis sent the bike and car back to Oakland on a big truck. Al didn't understand that Skip and Clarence were just letting off a little steam. The car and bike were toys they played with, but they're really not alone. Other players bring toys to camp, too.

George Beuhler was our right guard. He stands 6 feet 2, weighs 275 pounds, and is probably the strongest man on the team. George is an All-Pro but he has a habit of losing interest in the game. Sometimes the other linemen have to slap him around in the huddle to bring him back. "He does have a tendency to drift a bit," Gene Upshaw, our left guard says. "Yelling at him doesn't always work. He seems to have his mind on one hundred different things other than the game. It takes a good slap to get him concentrating again."

Our fullback, Pete Banaszak, tells about a particular game when we were behind and driving for a last minute go-ahead touchdown. Everyone was deadly serious as they listened to Kenny Stabler call the play. Then, all of a sudden, Beuhler started talking to Pete and asked, "Where'd you get those shoes? I've been thinking about changing mine and maybe I'll try a pair like yours. I like that fancy design."

We call George the "Mad Scientist" because he loves electronic gadgets. He made a little remote-controlled tank that he sends out to pick up the mail every morning. Once, I was sleeping and heard "RRRrrRRRrrrRR" coming down the hall. I got up to investigate and saw this tank coming toward my room. At first it scared the hell out of me, but then I realized it was only George's toy.

George likes remote-controlled airplanes, too. He used to let some of the other guys fly them until Pete Banaszak crashed one into a building. Now he won't let anyone touch his toys. George says. "You guys don't know how to use the controls."

Unfortunately, George doesn't know how to use the controls either. He brought a plane to practice one day. Everyone was in full gear preparing to scrimmage and George started flying his airplane around the field. The coaches told him to put the toy away but something was wrong with the controls. The plane started diving at us almost as though there were a nasty pilot flying it. Beuhler was punching the control box with his fist and cussing while everyone else was running around ducking and dodging. Finally, the gadget crashed into the goal post.

Someone screamed, "Beuhler, what the hell happened?"

He answered, "I lost contact!"

Skip and George are normal guys compared to Charley Philyaw. Charley's our 6–8 defensive end. We named him "King Kong." To say that Charley is sometimes a little slow catching on is an understatement. At practice, Charley hurt his hand and needed medical attention. He walked over to Pete Banaszak, holding his hand and asked, "Hey, man, what should I do?"

"Go see the doctor," Pete told him.

"The doctor?" Philyaw asked.

"Yeah, the doctor," Pete said.

Philyaw walked out into the middle of a pass defense drill and pulled Skip Thomas aside saying, "Man said I should show you this," and he stuck his bloody paw in Skip's face.

Coach Madden asked, "Philyaw, what are you doing?"

"Showing my hand to the doctor." Charley answered. "The man said that I should show it to the Doctor."

"Get that man the hell out of my sight!" Madden screamed.

Every morning the offense and defense go to separate film rooms and view game films. One morning, Philyaw was sitting in the offensive film room ten minutes before someone said, "Philyaw, you're in the wrong room."

Defensive coach Tom Dahms had a nice meeting going without Charley, and when someone said, "Coach, Philyaw isn't here," he answered, "Good!"

During a morning practice session, Philyaw sprained his ankle. He wasn't expected to practice for a couple of days, but that afternoon, like a good rookie, Philyaw was back on the field. Charley was wearing one shoe on his good foot and a sandal on the one he had sprained, but that wasn't all. Charley had on different colored socks, the wrong colored jersey, no belt, and his thigh pads were in upside down. Everyone stopped and stared in disbelief. This was a professional athlete? The coaches took Charley aside and started counting up the things wrong with his uniform. Philyaw set an NFL record. Ten things were wrong with his uniform.

There is, of course, a more serious side to our training camp. It's not all toys, mistakes, and laughs. For example, the bar bowling and air hockey tournaments are serious to the point of almost being sacred rituals.

Phil Villapiano is our All-Pro linebacker, but his finest hour did not occur on the football field. Phil established the air hockey and bar bowling tournaments and even the rules and regulations the games are governed by. "Foo," that's Phil's nickname, is the commissioner of the tournament. The man responsible for Phil's nickname is Duane Benson, another linebacker, who got so drunk one night during the tournament games that he couldn't pronounce "Phil." He kept on slobbering out, "Hey, Foo, he's cheatin.' "

"That's it," Foo shouted. "Everyone has to cheat! From now on, cheating is the cardinal rule of all tournaments!"

Up to that point, we only had one rule, and that was that all contestants had to be drunk. Every so often someone would fake a drunk act and try to get in the tournament and win. But when Art Thomas threatened to start giving urine tests to everyone to make sure all contestants were equally drunk, everyone started tipping their glasses. Like I said, the tournament is serious.

When Foo added the cheating rule, all the air hockey players started wearing long winter coats. The people of Santa Rosa thought it was a little strange, us wearing heavy coats in the middle of summer with the temperature over 100 degrees, but the long sleeves were great for deflecting shots. Some of the air hockey games would go on for hours and no one would score.

During the last week of camp we would hold our championship games, and the winners are driven through town in convertibles with a police escort. Foo sits in the first car and the champions follow behind. They throw candy out to the people that line the streets and make a parade out of it. The townspeople come out and wave and seem happy. I don't know if they're happy because of the parade or because our camp is just about over. The people of Santa Rosa really do act differently toward us when we are about to leave camp than they do when we first arrive. I've noticed that when we first come up to Santa Rosa, the townsfolk seem a little jumpy and somewhat paranoid. I've seen mothers hide their young daughters behind their dresses when we passed by, and you can see people peeking out of their homes from behind closed doors and windows. It all seems quite strange until I take a look at Skip's car, Beuhler's tank, or Philyaw bumping his head on the same low-hanging branch year after year. Then I understand.

Really, the Raiders have never done anything serious enough to warrant people being jumpy around us. Unless . . . well, there was this one time when the Coleco Company (they make the air hockey tables) decided to throw a party for the champions and the rest of the team. That was sort of a mistake on the management's part. Things were just fine when everyone was stuffing their faces with food, but then the management made their second mistake. Some Coleco Company official stood up, tapped his water glass with a fork, and said, "Gentlemen, may I have your attention?" I just shook my head because I knew it was bad timing. Nobody wanted to hear a speech. One of the guys threw a hot buttered roll at the man, hit him right smack in the head, and said, "Ah, shut up!"

Now that was funny. Someone else threw another roll and then another and another. It was getting hilarious. As the rolls began sailing all over the room, one of them hit the wife of a company vice president, and when she threw a dish of butter back at us, the war was on. Pies, green beans, paper cups, and drinks started flying around the room. Now, some people seemed to think all of that was uncalled-for behavior in a group of adults, but it was just what we expected at a banquet. After all, what's a banquet without a good fight? Still, though, the Coleco Company hasn't as yet had any more banquets for the Raiders.

I'm really starting to get ahead of myself. Here I am telling the story of the modern-day Raiders and I haven't given any history of the team. After all, the Oakland Raiders didn't wake up one morning and find themselves the type of organization they are presently. Just like anything worth having, it all started a long time ago and has taken countless hours of hard work.

For the trivia fans, the Raiders played their first game on a July night in 1960 against the Dallas Texans. With 4:27 left on the clock in the first quarter, a 190-pound running back named Buddy Allen broke off left guard and scored the Raiders' first touchdown. It seemed easy, but that was only the beginning of an uphill struggle that eighteen years later brought the Raiders their first and only Super Bowl Championship.

Although the Raiders went on to lose their first game, none of the 12,000 fans at Kezar Stadium could foresee that one of the most successful franchises in professional football had been born.

During their first three years the Raiders spent more time organizing and reorganizing the front office management than they did signing draft picks. Without quality athletes, game results did little to encourage team owners, and confidence within the locker room slipped to an all-time low. Everyone in the organization knew that something had to be done.

Before the start of the 1962 season, someone suggested "new blood" to restructure the organization. It was a great idea, and someone introduced the name of Al Davis, a then thirty-three-year-old, hippy-looking assistant on Sid Gillman's San Diego Chargers general staff. Davis had a genius for talking athletes away from the NFL and into signing with the Chargers. In a war between the two leagues, the AFL and NFL, Al Davis was the H-Bomb and commanded much respect.

Al Davis sounded like the man, although some thought that he was a little too aggressive for the Oakland organization and his "do-anything-to-win" tactics might give the team a bad image. But when the owners reasoned everything out, the image of a "loser" seemed much worse than the image of a "do-anything-to-win winner."

Al Davis was hired as the head coach and general manager and given complete control of the Raiders' future. His first day on the job was spent firing everyone from the ball boys to the ticket takers. His next actions concerned the football players themselves. The Raiders had a core of solid players to build around, but they needed new muscles in certain areas. Al weeded out every weak link and started to build anew.

Al Davis started training camp by saying, "Pride and poise! That's the answer! You're Oakland Raiders wherever you go; whatever you do. Anybody who is ashamed of that can get on a plane and leave right now. You're here to win! Win! Win!"

The door to the Oakland organization was swinging on new hinges, and the team started the season off with two home games in a row and two big wins. But when Al took the team east of the Mississippi, he ran into trouble. After three road games the Raiders were struggling along with a 2–3 record.

In every football game, and in every football season, there are points that can turn things either way. When the Raiders traveled to San Diego, few people gave them any chance of turning their losing ways around. After all, San Diego was the pride of the AFL and many people thought the Chargers could even beat any NFL team.

A capacity crowd filled Balboa Stadium, hoping that Oakland might field something that slightly resembled a professional football team—or, at the very least, the crowd hoped that the Raiders would make a game out of it, if only for a while.

The Raiders scored first, but the Chargers came back for a 10–7 lead at the end of the first quarter. In a matter of seconds the Raiders were back on top, 14–10.

The San Diego fans started screaming for Raider blood and the Chargers responded with 13 unanswered points. The rout was on, or so it seemed.

When the fourth quarter of action started, however, the scoreboard read: San Diego 23, Raiders 28. The Raiders had managed to score two touchdowns on the Chargers in the third period; one on a lucky interception and the other on a long pass play. It didn't matter to San Diego, because the Chargers were getting real serious.

San Diego started off with a field goal, and three plays later they had the ball again. This time Keith Lincoln broke away for a 51-yard scamper and the Chargers led 33–28.

With a little over one minute to play in the game, some of the San Diego fans made their way toward the exits. But back inside the concrete structure, on the grass field of Balboa Stadium, the Raiders were about to answer their first real test of pressure. Much to the dismay of the remaining Charger fans, the Raiders did not shrivel up and disintegrate. Patiently they moved the ball closer to the San Diego goal line. Then, with just seconds left and using what seemed like an almost cocky display of talent and strategy, the Raiders worked halfback Glenn Shaw behind defenders for the touchdown pass that historically capped the Raiders first come-from-behind win.

The Raiders were a growing organization, and Al Davis kept busy finding new ways to win. When Al started making personnel moves that bordered on brilliant, other teams suddenly became cautious of whom they traded to Oakland. Davis had a magical way of turning another team's scrap into All-Pro players.

With Buffalo, Al traded away three promising players for a so-so Archie Matsos. The promising players were soon forgotten while Matsos went on to All-League status as a lineman.

Several teams in the league had a good laugh when Al seemed to lose all reason and sanity by making a trade for Clem Daniels, a defensive back who wasn't. Everyone knew that Daniels was big, strong, and fast, but he couldn't cover receivers on pass patterns and he didn't know how to tackle running backs. Al wiped the smirks off everyone's face by making Clem a running back who rushed for over one thousand yards during his first year.

If that wasn't enough, Al then went out and made a hilarious deal with Houston for their aging running back Billy Cannon. Rumor had it that Cannon was washed up, and why Al Davis wanted him was beyond anyone's ability to understand. As the season started, everyone found out what Al Davis had known all the time. Billy Cannon wasn't fast enough for a running back but his size and strength made him an excellent tight end.

Next came the deal for Denver's tight end Hewritt Dixon, who was not a great blocker, ran poor pass patterns, and couldn't catch very well. Still, Al Davis made a deal for Dixon and turned the man into a fullback. Dixon became a tank that ran over defensive players. The essence of Al's success stemmed from the fact that he wasn't afraid to bring in washed-up players or so-called troublemakers. He was building a team, and judged a man solely by his talents and what he could do for the Raiders. As an Oakland Raider, I am given the flexibility to be myself. It's always been that way with the Raiders, and I like it. Nobody is ever prejudged by the cut of his hair, color of his skin, or his weight. Everyone in the Oakland organization is treated as a professional until his abilities or lack of abilities dictate otherwise. Maybe that's why you can look down our roster and see the names of several men who were losers with other teams but became winners with the Raiders.

There I go again, getting carried away. Before I get into the modern-day Raiders, there are still a few stories worth mentioning about the history of the team.

Within a few years the Raiders had established themselves as a winning team that came from behind with miraculous finishes. But there was still another chapter of the Raider story to be written.

December 31, 1967, the Raiders hosted the Houston Oilers for the American Conference Championship. By now, Al Davis had given up his coaching duties to John Madden and was acting as the team's general manager. He still hired and fired the players, but Madden's job was to keep the Raiders winning. In 1964, when Madden took over, he started teaching something just a little different in the way of defensive football. Madden's style was aggressive and punishing. Slowly, the team started to develop this style, too, and in the championship game against Houston, the Raiders were blazing away with all their big guns.

Although Gruesome Sunday started out innocently

enough with the Raiders getting a 37-yard field goal from a Houston cast-off, George Blanda, everything seemed to pick up from that point. The home crowd sensed the hostility and started screaming for blood. Before long, the Raiders were chewing at the jugular veins of the Houston Oilers. This was the other part of the Raider image that I was talking about, the ability to become brutal and violent to the point of being almost indecent. Houston was being raped of pride and sacrificed to the 50,000 Raider fans. The score totalled Raiders 40, Houston 7.

Then came Super Bowl II and the Green Bay Packers. Seasoned vets such as Bart Starr, Jim Taylor, Henry Jordan, Fuzzy Thurston, and the rest of the Packers knew their coach, Vince Lombardi, was going to retire after this game. They wanted to give him something special to remember. They did. The Raiders were handled rather easily, 33–14, but the game to them was more a direct violation of their motto, "Pride and Poise," than it was a disgrace. But even through the tears of disappointment, one thing was evident: The top was now in sight.

The next season the Raiders missed the Super Bowl as Joe Namath led the Jets down to Miami and beat the Colts 16–7 for the first AFL win ever. The Raiders had already earned a place in football history that particular year, however, by playing in the "Heidi Bowl."

Earlier in the season the New York Jets had come to Oakland for an important game, and NBC was there to televise the action, or at least part of the action. For some reason, the Raiders seemed to play their best in desperate situations, so they let the Jets get ahead 32–29 with only 1:05 left in the game. Everyone realized the Jets only had the lead and hadn't as yet won the game. It was going to be an exciting last minute of play, and football buffs from coast to coast settled down to watch.

Then, at 7:00 P.M. sharp, just as the Raiders took over the ball only seventy-nine yards from a touchdown, some wizard at the controls at NBC pressed a button and there was this little blonde girl prancing around a mountainside picking flowers. This was Heidi, the little girl that lived with her grandfather at the foot of the Jungfrau and ate goat cheese.

While the Raiders were moving the ball down the field, Heidi was dancing in the forests delighting the hearts of little children, while their fathers were melting NBC telephone lines with obscene calls. Even Julian Goodman, president of NBC, was on the phone trying to call his office and get the order in to restore the game. He was home watching the game, and even he wanted to see the ending. But all telephone lines coming into NBC were busy.

In the minute and five seconds it took Heidi to dance from her cottage to the fields of flowers, the Raiders had scored and were about to kick off to Namath and the Jets. There was just about enough time for someone to score yet another touchdown. Heidi was about to catch a butterfly as the Raiders kicked off and eleven men clad in silver and black went rumbling after the football. The ball had taken a few strange bounces, hit a couple of Jets, and went on into the end zone, where it was covered by the Raiders for a touchdown. As Heidi sat in the field watching a buttercup grow, NBC flashed the final score across the screen: Raiders 42, Jets 32.

The Raiders had that flair for last-minute excitement and they were a physical team, but there was still the Super Bowl Championship that had never found its way to Oakland, California. I guess it all comes down to those fragile harmonies between players, coaches, and general managers. I mean, that's what creates the outcomes of most games, but the Super Bowl is something else. I'm sure that Al Davis had looked over his team's record, the best in professional football, and tried to figure out why the Raiders had never won the Super Bowl and had had only one chance even to play for the championship.

There really isn't any proven way to win the Super Bowl. When Green Bay won two Super Bowl championships, Lombardi was a coach who believed in the basic play book drilled to perfection. Dallas achieved success with a formula of complex strategy. Miami used a crunching running game and the zone defense, while the Steelers bulldozed their way to the top with a front four.

Every professional football camp starts with people taking aim on winning the Super Bowl. Any team that starts their season thinking only about surviving isn't worth much, and their record will reflect their very own shortcomings. I know that the two purposes of our Raiders' training camp are to get us ready for the coming season and to work toward the championship. But still, it all comes back to people, your people, beating someone else's people. I believe that winning year after year is a matter of pride and poise, or as the Raiders' institutional letterhead reads: "Commitment to Excellence."

Still, I am sorry to say, in my opinion getting to the Super Bowl and winning defy logic and come down to a matter of luck. Most winning teams have similar basics. Winners have quarterbacks that are true leaders and can handle the pressure. There are also several other important areas evident in all winners, such as good pass protection as a matter of pride and will, a front line that will put pressure on the quarterback, and a tenacious secondary with someone just like me waiting to bust receivers. In addition, all winners have abusive running backs, speedy receivers, a solid kicking game, coaches that do not disintegrate under pressure, and management with vision.

When you get down to Super Bowl Sunday and you're playing for the championship, believe me, it's just a matter of luck. I'm not selling short the work and effort to get there, but when you have ten or twelve professional teams that start a season believing they can win, and they all go out and work toward a championship, it has to come down to a little luck. Luck can come your way in many different forms, and your good luck is usually the other team's bad luck. Say that one team has a great first string quarterback and he gets hurt. That's bad luck for the quarterback and his team but good luck for the men standing on the other side of the field. So injuries are good luck and bad luck. Luck in football isn't based on injuries alone. Luck can be someone clipping your free safety and the official not seeing the play. Luck can be recovering a fumble that an official said was a dead ball or catching a pass that should have been called an incompletion. What I'm really trying to say is that because of the high level of competition, it takes luck to win the Super Bowl even though your every effort, dream, and desire might tell you it was hard work paying off.

In 1972 our record was 10–3–1, and we ended the season with six impressive wins. Al Davis said, "This is the best Raider team in the history of the organization."

We had our sights on the Super Bowl, but in Pittsburgh we ran into a team with the same objective and working just as hard as the Raiders. The Steelers had won their first division championship ever and we felt that a 0–1 record in post-season play would be nice for our friends in Pittsburgh. The Steelers, however, had other ideas, and the game was a war with the final results resting on one second of playing time and luck.

Three Rivers Stadium was brand new, and the Steelers felt they should give the hometown fans something to cheer about. They came out for action in a surly mood, especially the defensive line with L. C. Greenwood, Joe Green, Ernie Holmes, and Dwight White taking turns smashing our quarterback, Daryle Lamonica, into the turf and batting his passes down his throat. The Steelers' defense was so nasty that Daryle was saying Hail Marys as he broke the huddle and thanking God for working a small miracle every time he completed a pass.

The game wasn't a runaway, because we also have a defensive team that can get nasty. And so, on that particularly warm December day in Pittsburgh, the air around the stadium exploded from the sonic booms of bone-shattering tackles. For fifty-seven minutes of playing time, the game was all defense, with the exception of two field goals by Pittsburgh's Roy Gerela. I believe the score might have ended 6–0 if it hadn't been for the last-minute heroics of our third-string quarterback, Kenny "Snake" Stabler, who was called into action with only a few minutes left to play and eighty yards between him and a touchdown.

The Snake was cool and answered the pressure of the

partisan crowd and the Steelers by moving our team right down the field. With a first down and ten on the Steelers' thirty yard line, Snake dropped back to pass and noticed a safety blitz. He calmly tucked the ball under his arm and twisted and slithered his way down the side line and into the end zone, unmolested by the Steelers. If the Steelers were wondering about Kenny's nickname, "Snake," before his thirty yard run, they all knew why after he finished scoring. From his college playing days at Alabama, Kenny had been called "Snake." His college coach, Mr. Paul "Bear" Bryant, once said, "Why, Kenny's harder to get ahold of than a river snake."

Well, anyway, Blanda kicked the extra point and the good guys were on top. It seemed like another come-from-behind victory, but the Steelers had other ideas. When you get into a game with top-notch professionals and your team is only one point ahead, it's really not over. Sometimes, there is more football played in the last few minutes of desperation than in three quarters of blood, sweat, pain, and punishment.

Only 1:13 remained in the game as quarterback Terry Bradshaw brought the Steelers up to the line. With the right play calling, the Steelers could run eight, maybe ten, plays. I was hoping they would let Bradshaw call his own plays. That way the Steelers could only run one or two plays before the game was over. Bradshaw isn't known for his imagination.

Terry started off by flipping a nine yard pass to Frenchy Fuqua and came back with a draw play to Franco Harris that covered another nine yards. I knew right then that someone was calling the plays from the sideline.

On the next two plays, Bradshaw tried passing in my area. The first pass was a good one and I was lucky to get my hand on the ball and deflect it away from the receiver. The second pass was a copy of a Daryle Lamonica Hail Mary attempt. Bradshaw was running around trying to avoid our people and he just put the ball in the air for anyone to grab. I nearly intercepted. With third and ten facing the Steelers, Bradshaw went up top again, and again I nearly intercepted. The Steelers had one more chance: it was do or die.

Bradshaw dropped back into a pocket and looked up in time to see our defensive line blotting out the sunlight with a tremendous pass rush. Without looking upfield, Bradshaw flung another prayer pass just as one ton of silver-and-black-clad bodies smashed him to the ground. By this time Frenchy Fuqua had broken into a little curl pattern over the middle. I dropped off a few steps and timed my hit to arrive in Frenchy's back just about the same time the ball was going to arrive in his hands. I wanted to smash one more Steeler before the final gun went off, and the Frenchman was my target. I didn't think Frenchy could catch my helmet in his back and still hang on to the ball, so I never gave a thought about going for the interception. I blasted into Frenchy with a full head of speed and the ball bounced off us and sailed twenty yards back downfield. George Atkinson and some of the other players came over to me and we were jumping around celebrating. They were all congratulating me for breaking up the pass, getting Frenchy to go limping off the field in a daze, and, of course, winning the game. That, we all were sure, was the Steelers last gasp. But like I said, after I hit Frenchy, the ball sailed twenty yards back up the field. It just so happened that Franco Harris, outside the action, was heading over toward the sideline when the ball plopped into his hands. And what does Franco usually do when he gets the ball? He runs out of bounds if the defense is near him or he runs for the end zone if it's wide open. Hell, with the Raiders jumping all over each other because they won the game, it was a wide open freeway to the end zone, and Franco covered seventy yards like a '56 Buick with mudflaps and a coon tail hanging from the mirror.

Five seconds were still on the clock when Franco stepped into the end zone as a hero but the screaming and cussing lasted longer, much longer. The Raiders' staff was screaming that the ball had hit Frenchy and it was an illegal play. On the other side of the field, the Steelers swore up and down that I hit the ball first and it was a legal play.

The ruling is that a ball cannot touch two consecutive offensive players and remain in play for the offense. If the ball even nicks a defensive man, and then the offensive man catches it, it is a legal play. The Raiders felt that the ball bounced off Frenchy into the waiting arms of Franco. The Steelers believed the ball hit me first and then Franco caught it. Me and Frenchy? Well, Frenchy wasn't in any condition to honestly judge who the ball hit or even what hit him. When the reporters asked Frenchy if the ball did hit him, all he could say was, "Damn, that sucker really hit me! I didn't know where the hell I was or even who I was, and you're asking me about the ball?" As for myself, I couldn't honestly say if the ball hit me. I wasn't worried about the ball at the time. I just wanted to lay some wood on Frenchy and I did.

The play was so close that even after we viewed the game films with stop action, nobody could tell who the ball hit on that moment of impact. But to this very day, because of my angle of attack and the position of Frenchy's body, I think it was an illegal play.

Referee Fred Swearingen was standing six or seven yards away from the play and he ruled it legal and signaled touchdown. Still, even he must have felt ill at ease over the quick decision and called for a time-out. The officials huddled together in the end zone and tried to figure out what happened, while both benches were screaming and cussing at each other. Swearingen then ran over to the dugout phone and called Art McNally, supervisor of officials, who happened to be sitting in the press box, and asked for a decision. Ten minutes later, after the home town crowd started getting a little restless, Swearingen ran back out onto the field and signaled touchdown for the second time in fifteen minutes.

There are advantages to the home field, and I'm sure the Steelers were enjoying theirs. If the game had been played in Oakland, that play would have gone down as an incompleted pass and we would have enjoyed our home-field advantage. So when all things are equal, you need a little luck to get you through to the Super Bowl and at that time and place, the Steelers had it going for them. Don't get the idea I'm basing the success of professional football teams solely on luck because that's not true. I'm just saying that when teams have equal strengths, Lady Luck will usually decide the game results.

I know better than anyone that the Raiders have won their share of games on luck. For example, in 1973 and 1974 the Miami Dolphins won back-to-back Super Bowls. In 1975 the Dolphins didn't make it to the Super Bowl, because of the Raiders and one lucky play. On a last second, falling-down pass play, Kenny Stabler got off a touchdown pass a split second before he was tackled.

In 1976 we got by New England and advanced in the play-offs, again with a last-second touchdown pass. That one pass play was the difference between us watching the Super Bowl and winning the Super Bowl. New England had us down 21–17, with less than a minute to go in the game. Stabler tried hitting Cliff Branch in the corner of the end zone, but the pass was high and it looked as though we were finished. That was our last play. Then one of the officials caught Sugar Bear Hamilton hitting Kenny after the play and we had new life. From there, it was a touchdown and a big win. The next week we trampled the Steelers 24–7 and started looking forward to the Super Bowl and the Vikings.

I know that coaches and players alike believe in luck, and Al Davis, John Madden, and the Raiders are no exception to that rule. The only trouble is that the Raiders carry their luck charms and superstitions a little too far. I'm talking about Coach Madden and Al Davis for the most part because they really seem to sail off the deep end when it comes to mumbo-jumbo.

I guess the superstitious phases of Raider mania hit the hardest a few years back when fifteen or sixteen of the guys wanted to play in a golf tournament instead of practicing. Coach Madden understood, I guess, because the guys went golfing. Then, on Sunday, we smashed the New York Giants, 42–0. That just happened to be the most points we scored all season and the only shutout the defense recorded. Now Coach

Madden encourages the guys to go golfing and even started a special team golfing tournament.

The golfing tournament is simple compared to the many other superstitious beliefs the Raiders hold to. It's just like throwing salt over your left shoulder for good luck (and Al Davis does that all the time) or the team not traveling on the thirteenth day of the month. Now, superstitions include eating the same pregame meal (if we won the last game), staying at the same hotel, and coaches wearing the same clothes. If we lose, then everything changes.

In Denver we always stayed at the Continental Hotel and we always beat Denver and we always won our division championship. I guess the Denver management also has some superstitious blood in them because they took over the Continental and moved us out. The team never really liked staying there anyway. It was an old, cinder block building, drafty and cold, and not my idea of upper-middle-class living. But Al Davis insisted that we beat Denver because we stayed at the Continental. This past season, when Denver took over the hotel, Al fought to keep us there, but the management of the place said we had to go. Last season Denver beat us twice and won the Division title for the first time in the history of their club. Al Davis went around scowling at everyone and saying, "I told you so!"

I didn't believe in that sort of witchcraft, but then we went to San Diego for a game. Strange things started to happen. In the past we stayed at the Star Dust Motel and the Chargers hadn't beaten us in sixteen games. As a matter of fact, San Diego couldn't muster enough points on the scoreboard to make the games respectable. But this past season, for some unknown reason, the Chargers' general staff decided to move their team into the Star Dust and they shifted us over to the Hylanda. I don't know if superstition spurred the move or not but we were quartered on the other side of town and San Diego had our winning motel.

Al Davis and John Madden were upset over the deal, but it didn't shake up any of the players. We still went on with a normal pregame night (five wild parties) and showed up at the stadium early Sunday afternoon in time for the kick-off. The game was simply unbelievable. The Chargers won, 12–10. After that experience, every member on the team started to avoid stepladders, black cats, and new hotels. Every pregame burp and sneeze became a new ritual.

Speaking of rituals, I've always let Skip tape my forearms before a game. It has nothing to do with good luck charms or superstitions. I hit people in the head with my forearms, and the tape provides me with some protection. Now the coaches come over to Skip and make sure he's going to tape my forearms.

Several years back, some of the coaches would frown on Skip screaming and cussing in the locker room before a game. Skip wasn't mad at anyone, he just likes to cuss. On one rare occasion, Skip didn't cuss and the locker room felt empty. We went out on the field and proceeded to get our heads beaten in by a funky Cleveland team, 7–3. Now everyone does his share, and it doesn't take much to keep Skip in the right frame of mind and cussing.

In spite of everything, the Raiders are the winningest club in professional football. I guess it comes down to Spirit. I'm not talking about ghosts or goblins. I'm referring to the camaraderie that develops among people working together as a team. I have built many friendships with my Raider teammates that I know will endure long after our football playing days are over. This is much more important to me than all the money I've made or the fame I have achieved. Unfortunately, however, friendships can sometimes lead to some very sticky, yet humorous, entanglements.

One time, we were playing in Pittsburgh and Clarence Davis came up to my room with a big smile on his face. He said, "Tate, I just gave an interview for you."

"Meaning what?" I asked.

Clarence started explaining with a smirk on his face, "You remember the time we went out to dinner in Oakland and you left me? Remember, Tate? Remember that time when you left with that big dude's lady friend?"

I remembered what C.D. was talking about. One

time, when he and I went out to dinner, I noticed this nice-looking lady sitting across from us staring and smiling at me. Well, she got up to powder her nose and I just happened to get up to make a phone call or something, I just don't remember. Anyway, I talked with her in the lobby and we both decided to leave together. She left her boy friend and I left C. D.

"Damn, C. D., I hope you didn't get upset about me sticking you with the check for dinner," I replied.

"Oh, no, Tate, I wasn't angry about the check I got stuck with. The lady's friend had a knife and he wanted to stick me with it. I was lucky to get away with my life so I decided to do you a favor. That's why I gave an interview for you."

C. D. was excited. I knew that he must have really stuck it to me, so I asked, "Okay, tell me about it."

"Well, Tate, I was down in the lobby just minding my own business when this man comes up to me and starts asking questions. It was strange, though, because he kept calling me 'Mr. Tatum.' "

I knew what had happened. A lot of times reporters and even fans mistake Clarence and me. Really, though, I can't see the resemblance. I'm much better looking.

The man who came up to C. D. was a reporter and he wanted to interview me. He asked C. D., "Tell me, Jack, what receiver of the Steelers do you fear the most?"

C. D. answered, "Steelers' receivers! Ain't none of them worth a damn."

Obviously, the reporter was startled at my arrogant display of verbal abusiveness or, I should say, at C.D.'s. The man asked a second question. "Tell me, Jack, what do you think of the Steelers' running backs?"

"Chicken, all of them, chicken," C.D. replied.

The reporter was really taken in and he started firing questions at C.D.

"Do you have any respect for anyone on the Steelers' club?" the reporter asked.

"Mister, if I told you the Steelers were gutless suckers, that would be a compliment. Ain't none of the Steelers worth a damn, and tomorrow, me, Mr. Jack

Tatum, will personally beat them all over the stadium. You can quote me on that," Clarence told the man.

The man did quote him, and the Steelers read the story. Let me tell you, I had a hell of a time explaining everything to the few friends I did have on the Steelers' club.

Another time, I ended up with four armed bodyguards just because I was friends with George Atkinson. Some people say that George plays a little dirty; other people believe that George plays a little dirty; and still others don't like dirty football players. Because I play next to George, and we are good friends, the people who say nasty things about George believe the same about me. I'm really innocent but I'm considered guilty by association.

One time, this not-too-happy Pittsburgh Steeler fan thought George had roughed up Lynn Swann. That wasn't so very bad for me but when the same man started writing letters to the Raiders front office mentioning my name right beside George's and also the fact that he was going to blow us off the face of the world, I became upset. Still, though, I wasn't really worried until they caught the man planting a bomb in the Oakland bus station with "George and Jack" painted on it. The man knew we were leaving town to go east for a game with the Steelers and he figured he'd get us as we passed by the locker in the bus station. George and I both rationalized that the man was of low mentality, suffering from perverted and degenerate tendencies (obviously a Steeler fan), and certainly nothing to worry about. Raider management, however, felt it was serious and assigned four armed bodyguards for George and myself. We pleaded with Coach Madden, "The man was just a nut and you can't take him seriously. We don't even travel by bus, and if he was waiting for us at the bus station, he would have waited the rest of his life." It didn't do any good. For our trip to Pittsburgh, we had the company of armed bodyguards.

After it was all over, George and I talked about the man waiting at the bus station and why he would do such a dumb thing. We just couldn't figure it out, and then George said, "Maybe that's how the Steelers travel. Who knows?"

Sometimes, being a Raider can be rewarding, while other times it all becomes a serious problem and even embarrassing. A few years ago, we played in Washington, D.C., against the Redskins. It started off with a late flight into the nation's capitol and an evening meal. The team had made arrangements for us to eat at the hotel, and to start with, a salad bar was set up. Everyone was hungry after the flight except for Skip. He was hungry before the flight and during the flight; in fact, Skip is always hungry. But this time it was really bad. Skip was cussing and bitching before he got on the plane. The sandwiches he ate during the flight were not filling and he swore all the way across the country and into the hotel dining room. After all of that, Skip was going to eat. He walked up to the salad bar and started cussing at the top of his voice, "What the hell is this? Rabbit food? I'm a man and ain't gonna eat this damn rabbit food!"

Skip was screaming and people stopped eating. I could see lower jaws banging off china plates. We tried to pretend that Skip wasn't with us, that he just wandered in here by mistake. But sometimes you can't ignore Skip. I mean he has a way of using profanity that will capture your attention. Someone said, "Hey, Skip, keep it down!" That did it. Skip really started cussing. The hotel management rushed out with a couple of steaks and the rare meat managed to slow Skip down for a while.

After a light practice the next day, we decided to go on a tour of the White House. Actually, Al Davis had made arrangements for us to see the White House and meet the President. Al made those plans honestly believing that Skip would refuse to go. But hell, Skip was all fired up and cussing to get going. He wanted to meet the President. Now we had a problem. How do you tell Skip he can't cuss in the White House and in front of the President? Well, Madden and Davis had a meeting with Skip before we left the hotel and Skip just wasn't Skip. All during the tour he stood there with his arms folded and bottom lip sticking out and didn't say a word. The only time Skip ever gets that quiet is when he watches TV after the channels have all signed off. It was a nice tour and when it was over, Skip finally spoke. He said, "HELL, if a man can't cuss, ain't hardly no sense to be alive."

I once, just once, went out to an expensive French restaurant with Skip. We had dinner at Robert's in San Francisco and it was different. When the waiter brought the wine, he poured Skip a little in a fancy crystal glass. Skip slid the glass my way and said, "I never drink from a glass," and took a slug right out of the bottle. Then he said, "Damn, that's good wine. Bring us each a bottle but no glasses."

Another time, I made a mistake and went out with Skip before a game in Pittsburgh. We went to a disco in the Parkway Pavillion and Skip started getting loud and he set up the bar a few times. As the evening went on, Skip set up the bar a few more times and pretty soon everyone was falling-down drunk. From that point on, it was just a matter of time before Skip had everyone laughing and cussing at the top of their voices. The people just went crazy and Skip was right there leading them in the howling and screaming and cussing. After a few more "drinks for everyone" and about one thousand cuss words (that's just one normal sentence for Skip), the owner of the Parkway asked Skip about the heavy bill he was running up. Skip said, "Don't worry brother, I got it covered," and he went back to screaming and cussing. Then the owner asked him to slow down a little and Skip got up-tight and left without paying the bill. Just about that time, the drunken crowd started turning a little mean and when everyone found out that Skip had split without paying the bill, they were all looking for someone, anyone, to punch around. When a big dude pointed at me and said, "He's one of them," I decided to find the exit.

It was a good thing that our attorney, Tony DeCello, lives in Pittsburgh and he knew the owner of the Parkway. Otherwise, Skip and I would have listened to the game from the Pittsburgh jailhouse.

When I think about Skip, Clarence, George, and my other friends and teammates, I'm really proud to be a

Raider. I know that most of the guys aren't playing with a full deck, but these guys are real. Any one of them would give you the shirt off his back or his last dollar bill. I guess that makes them better men than most of the phony people running around the streets today. So, when the summer comes along, I sort of look forward to going up to Santa Rosa and the start of camp.

In 1976, when I left Oakland for camp, I was looking forward to the season more than at any other time in my career. I had a good feeling that this was the year the Raiders were going to do it. It was strange because everyone coming into camp honestly felt the same as I did even though nothing had really changed. The coaches were plotting secret plays and the players were rushing into new areas of foolishness but that is the way an Oakland Raider training camp always starts. Players can't get serious the first or second week of camp, and smart coaches realize that Super Bowl Champions are built over the course of a season.

When Foo (Villapiano) arrived in camp, he had a fantastic inspiration. He was going to find a Queen to reign over the Air Hockey Championships. Foo said, "But she's got to be ugly, ugly, ugly."

Foo came up with the lady after many hours of interviews and elimination contests. He sure can pick 'em. The lady accepted the honor of being our Queen and we held a special coronation. Kick-'em-in-the-head Hendricks, so named because of his favorite maneuver during a game, built a throne from old crates on the back of his pickup truck and drove Her Royal Majesty up and down the streets of Santa Rosa. If anyone had failed to notice before, then after Kick-'em was finished, the entire population of Santa Rosa knew for certain that the Raiders were back in town!

Meanwhile, back at the El Rancho Motel, our headquarters, Beuhler was busy with his erector set building a new tank, Philyaw was searching in vain for the doctor, and Skip was cussing. It seemed as though nothing had really changed. That was until someone came up with a new nickname for Beuhler: "Fog."

Nicknames are also an important part of Raider life. Getting your nickname is a sign that you've finally been accepted into the club. For example, most of the guys call Coach Madden "Big Red." Madden is a burly guy with red hair, but for some reason Skip calls him "Pinky."

Nobody is given a nickname; one must earn his title, even Skip. Most of the time we let ourselves go at training camp. We hardly shave and we never wear fancy clothes. After all, nobody is going to see us except the coaches and maybe the Queen. And who wants to look good for her? One day, Skip was walking over to the practice field looking the way he thought a Raider athlete should look. His appearance was bad even by Raider training-camp standards. Someone said that Skip looked as though he was coming back from one of his frequent trips to Mars and all points beyond. Bob Brown, a big offensive tackle, saw Skip coming up the path and jumped back ten steps and said, "Damn, Skip, you look like death warmed over, swallowed down whole, and spit back out." Skip looked terrible, but the next day he looked even worse. After a week of letting himself go, Skip earned the name "Dr. Death."

Everyone who's been through the wars has a nickname. My friends call me "The Reverend," not "The Assassin." They know that I am a saintly person on the field, but George Atkinson is the "Weasel." George gets himself into impossible situations but has a knack for weaseling his way out.

Some of the guys like to use their mouths a lot. Gene Upshaw, our All-Pro guard, is the "Pelican Jaw." He fancies himself a politician and keeps his jaw moving talking about the issues. Dave Rowe likes to hear himself talk, too. We call him, "Radio Rowe."

All-Pro wide receiver Cliff Branch has run the hundred in 9.2 seconds. Naturally, Cliff is the "Rabbit."

Neal Colzie, our punt return specialist, thinks he's a ladies' man. We call him "Sweet Pea."

Dave Casper is the "Ghost." Dave is the whitest white person I've ever seen. At the opposite end of the color spectrum is "Black Angus." Football fans know him as Art Shell, All-Pro tackle. Mark Van Eeghen isn't black, but his kinky afro hair style started the rumor about his mother running off with a black man.

Most of the time, we call Mark "Black Blood," but if he doesn't crack a smile with that nickname, we come back with "Bundini Brown, Jr." Skip says that Bundini and Mark look alike.

Clarence Davis is another man with two nicknames. Most of the time, we refer to him as "C. D.," but the bigger guys on the team call him the "Militant Midget." C. D. is only about 5 feet 9, and when people get on him about being short, he starts making threats about the little people taking over the world and shooting everyone over 5 feet 10.

If you're going to have nicknames, you must hit Al Davis with one, too. Everyone did call Al a variety of different names behind his back, but no one said anything to his face. As the general manager, Al is the man who handles contracts and the money. It's not that anyone treated Al like a special person, because he's really not, and doesn't put on any airs, but the players had this unwritten law to simply ignore the man. Treat him like he wasn't there until it was time for contract talks. But one night Skip forgot his wallet in the locker room and we drove back to pick it up. Al was in the weight room working out with his skinny arms. Skip started blasting on Al's physique and it was a heavy scene. Al rebutted with, "Skip, we're both the same size. You wear a size 44 suit and so do I." The next day at practice, to prove his point, Al came out dressed in a suit, size 44. Seeing how Al is more at home in a size 40, the jacket and pants fit a little loose. That's all Skip needed. Skip ran over and grabbed Al by the seat of the pants and started poking fun at the baggy suit. Skip was carrying on something terrible, and before long everyone was on the ground laughing, including Al. Finally, after Skip had nearly tugged Al's pants off, he blurted out "El Bago!" and now, even Al Davis had a nickname.

I admit that the Raiders do some strange things at a training camp, but there is also much time invested in serious work. The summers around Santa Rosa get blistering hot. I've seen the temperature soar to over 100 degrees, and when you're wearing heavy equipment and undergoing physical stress, it really gets hot. I've tasted my own salty perspiration and worked my body until I couldn't move, but it's all part of the game and the price you pay. To win football games you have to be in top physical condition, and there is only one way to get in shape: work until you can't take another step and then run the last hundred yards full speed.

We practice about four hours a day. Some people might think a four hour day would be a snap, but those people would be dead wrong. When you get into the grueling work of summer training camp, you need nicknames, tanks, and Philyaws just to keep your sanity.

Charles Philyaws is going to be one hell of a football player someday. But even if Philyaws wasn't a great athlete, I think the Raiders would have kept him around for at least the summer training camp. Charles was good for the team.

On his way to practice, Philyaw stepped in a hole and sprained his ankle. He limped his way through the day and late that night came over to our room to see the doctor. Philyaw was standing in the hallway outside our room, all 6 feet 9 inches of him, explaining his problem to Skip. Philyaw was saying, "Trainer say to get the whirlpool from you."

"What you talkin' about, Dummy?" Skip screamed at Philyaw.

"Trainer said you have the whirlpool and I need it for my ankle," Philyaw explained as he started taking off his shoe to show Skip the swollen ankle.

Skip turned to me for help and asked, "Tate, what's this big dummy talkin' about?"

I just shrugged my shoulders and rolled over in bed. I wasn't about to get mixed up in any of Skip's and Philyaw's communication problems.

Skip slammed the door in Philyaw's face and stormed over to the phone. He called the trainer and cussed the man out. Skip wanted someone, anyone, to teach Philyaw the difference between the team's doctor and the team's cornerback. Skip didn't stop with a phone call to the trainer either. He called Big Red, El Bago, Tom Dahms, and even one of the owners. Skip cussed and screamed for over an hour, but that was the last time Philyaw came after Skip for medical attention.

Next day at practice, Philyaw came over to Skip and said, "Hey, man, you know, all this time I's been thinking you were the doctor. Can you believe that?"

Every team has someone almost like Philyaw or "Fog" and even *something* similar to Skip. That only goes to prove that no team can base success or failure on reason and sanity. I agree in part with Paul Zimmerman, the Raiders are the flakiest team in professional football, but the Raiders are also the winningest team in professional football. To sit down and try to figure out the anatomy of a winner is impossible. There's really no way of getting inside the individuals and breaking everything down into easily understood terms. Football players defy logic, and the Raiders most of all. But one thing is for certain, when the official sets the ball for play and blows the whistle, something pulls all the talents, luck charms, superstitions, and personalities into a working unit directing all energies at one purpose: Winning! That's the way we started out in 1976.

The 1976 season was highlighted by several key games. Our first encounter with the Steelers was important because it set the stage for the rest of the season. Although we lost the verbal battle with the Steelers, our 31–28 come-from-behind win put us at 1 and 0, while the Steelers' record was quite the opposite.

Early in the season, because of injuries to key personnel, we had some very close games but were sporting a 3 and 0 record when we arrived in New England. That day New England was hot and the outcome was a humiliating 48–17 beating. You don't lose a game 48–17 and start talking about the Super Bowl unless you're an Oakland Raider. Normal people after getting beaten so badly start thinking about picking up the pieces, but not us. That defeat marked the point when we got serious and decided to make a determined effort at the number one spot in professional football.

During the course of the season, it often works out that one Sunday a team can be your bitter enemy and the next week root for you to win. Well, that's exactly what happened with the Raider-Steeler rivalry. After losing to us, the Steelers started to look pathetic. After five games they had only managed one win, and the chance of their repeating as Super Bowl contestants was highly in doubt. The pure truth was that they needed a miracle finish to even make the play-offs. The season came down to this: Cincinnati had a one-game lead on the Steelers in their division. If the Bengals were to win their last two games, it wouldn't matter what Pittsburgh did, because Cincinnati would be the division champs. However, if the Bengals lost one of their remaining two games and Pittsburgh won both of their contests, then the Steelers, with a record identical to the Bengals', would be awarded the Central Division Championship by virtue of having beaten Cincinnati twice during the year. It was safe to assume the Bengals would beat their last opponent of the season, the Jets, but their other remaining game was against us. Because the Steelers had done a complete turnaround and were playing the best football in the NFL, some folks naturally assumed the Raiders would lay down, let the Bengals beat us, and prepare for the play-offs. That way the Pittsburgh Steelers would have been eliminated from any play-off hopes, making the road to Super Bowl XI much easier for us or any other team.

Once again the Oakland Raiders became the topic of many discussions in the Steel City, but this time it was "Hooray for Oakland!" The Steelers, their fans, and all the news media in and around Pittsburgh tried everything from shame tactics to a praise-laden, positive-thinking approach to get us in a winning mood for our forthcoming game with the Bengals. Some said that the Raiders were men and because of our pride we would go out and beat the Bengals. Some people accused us of being scared to death of the Steelers and predicted we would lay down and let Cincinnati beat us. People in the street, newspaper men, and television reporters in Pittsburgh all had their own ideas of what might happen on the Monday night when ABC came to Oakland for the showdown game between the good guys and the Bengals.

If you were to look at everything on paper, the Raiders were a better team, but anything can happen during a football game. The Bengals came into town thinking about winning, I'm sure, and maybe even a few of them

actually thought we were scared of the Steelers. Those
who felt that way failed to realize that any winning organization is built on a deep-rooted pride, a pride that
makes good teams great. Yes, the Steelers were playing
excellent football and were quite possibly the best team
in football. Then again, the Raiders hadn't exactly been
playing shoddy football themselves. For anyone to assume we were scared of the Steelers was simply absurd.
And for any coach, player, fan, or reporter to think
that we would lay down and let the Bengals win was
ricidulous. It just so happens that I believe the Raiders
are the best team in football, and I enjoy proving that
point every Sunday or Monday night.

When you honestly believe you are the best in any
profession, you do not shy away from a challenge; you
seek out the best of the competition to test your talents
against. Sure, Cincinnati had the potential to "get
lucky" and beat us, but it would be a most difficult task.
As Oakland Raiders, my teammates and I had no need
of any of the Steeler psychology to get us ready for the
Bengals. To go on to win the Super Bowl without facing Pittsburgh again would have been a very shallow
victory indeed. But to blast Cincinnati away and trample
everyone who got in the way of our rush to become
number one, well, that is what our motto, "Pride and
Poise," is all about. It's all a part of becoming a man
and being called a professional. To hide from any player or team is cowardice. If I had felt the Raiders were
going to lay down, I would have asked to sit this one out.
Maybe I would have even asked to be traded. Never in
my career have I ever approached a football game or
anything with the thought of letting the other team win.
When Monday night came along, I am proud to say
that every member on the Raider team and staff went
out onto the field with a ruthless attitude toward the
Bengals.

Simply winning the game was not our intention: We
wanted something between slaughter and annihilation.
It all came down to the fact that we believed the Steelers could offer us the best competition, and every member on the Raiders team wanted to give the Steelers

every chance in the world to back up their mouths with some play-off action. All year long we heard about "criminals" and "cheap-shot artists" and "lucky Raiders" coming from Pittsburgh, and for some strange reason, we assumed those remarks were directed toward Oakland. A play-off game with Pittsburgh would be good for the teams, the league, the fans, and the reputation of football itself. With that special incentive, believe me, no one connected with the Raider organization even considered lying down for the Bengals.

I shouldn't say that Cincinnati was outclassed, but midway into the second period we were sporting a 21–0 lead and everyone started going for the throat. Although the final score ended up 34–21, the thirteen-point spread was no indication of the real beating we gave Cincinnati. I don't know what the sports fans thought about us before the game, but I'm sure that even Pittsburgh fans across the country must have found a thread of respect to cling to when considering the type of men who wear the silver and black of Oakland.

When the season ended, because of our win over the Bengals, Pittsburgh was in the play-offs. Although both Pittsburgh and Oakland had different opponents for the semifinals of the American Conference, it was a good bet we would meet in Oakland for the championship. While we were busy with New England on Saturday afternoon, Pittsburgh was traveling to Baltimore for their Sunday encounter.

Our game with New England was highlighted with a typical Raider finish. We were losing 21–17 with less than one minute to play as Stabler began marching the silver and black machine down the field. As usual, Stabler moved the offensive unit into the end zone as the clock was ticking off the last few seconds. It was a 24–21 win for the Raiders.

On Sunday Pittsburgh proved they were one of the best teams in the NFL as they ran off 41 unanswered points. The Colts were never in the game.

After Pittsburgh's game the television cameras went inside the Steeler locker room for some interviews about the game and next week's affair in Oakland. Most of the

Steelers expressed optimism about their chances against us, which was to be expected, but then they interviewed Franco. I was shocked to hear Franco say, "I can hardly wait for next week. I want to beat the hell out of those son-of-a-bitches."

Obviously, he was referring to the Oakland Raiders, but I couldn't figure out how he was going to back up that rather stiff statement. I'm sure Steeler fans really felt Franco was their main man because of his brassy attitude toward the Raider menace, but saying something and backing it up are very different. Verbally, Franco was seriously threatening Cosell's crown, but there was always Sunday and the championship game for him to put his lip against my Hook. I was thinking, of course, about our past experiences with "Sideline Harris." He had not been what you might call a physical force to be reckoned with in any of those games, but maybe now, after all these years, he was wearing different colors. Sunday was to be a day where many questions would be answered.

As the drama began to unfold during the course of the week, it became obvious why Franco could make so daring a pre-game statement about the individuals in Oakland. It seems he hurt his ribs in the Baltimore game and wasn't even going to suit up for his "I-can-hardly-wait" encounter with the Raiders. We all know how disappointed Franco was, but he'll never realize just how sad it made the Raider defense feel when we learned he would not be in there slipping and sliding his way through eleven sons-of-bitches.

Later in the week Franco assured the press he would be ready for the game, but I knew those were only words into the wind. The reality of Sunday afternoon was that Pittsburgh would be without Franco and Rocky Bleier. Rocky had injured his foot during the Baltimore game, and although he wanted to play, it was simply a physical impossibility. I knew that without Rocky clearing a path to the sidelines for Franco, the Steelers were going to lose their punch in the running game, but they still had their great defense.

Before the game the press had worked over the

cheap-shot angle and predicted the Steelers were going to get George and me, but that was only the press talking. It was also said that the game was going to be a grudge match because of the hatred that existed between the two teams, but that was only trash used to take up space in the newspapers. Both teams, I was sure, were going to get serious on Sunday, but I don't think that even Ray Mansfield was thinking about taking a cheap shot.

When everything was over, I was sorry the Steelers didn't offer us more competition. We won the game rather easily, 24–7. I'm sure that injuries had taken something away from Pittsburgh, but even their defense wasn't tough. Our offensive team was able to run, pass, and probably could even have walked over Pittsburgh. It just wasn't the type of championship game a fan wants to see or an athlete wants to be part of. But when it was over, I think everyone realized the Raiders at that particular time, even though the Super Bowl was weeks away, were the best team in football.

On Sunday, January 9, 1977, the Oakland Raiders met the Minnesota Vikings in Super Bowl XI. The Raiders were a physical team and the Vikings were a passive one. That was the first indication it wasn't going to be a great Super Bowl game. Also, the Vikings had several tendencies that could only hurt their chances against a team such as Oakland. For example, Tarkenton isn't a drop-back passer. Because of his size (he's only 5 feet 11), he rolls out slightly. This enables him to see the field of play better than if he stood back in a pocket while defensive giants blotted out the sunlight.

Tark's little roll out would be ineffective against us because we could rush our ends from the outside in passing situations. Since our defensive ends range from 6 feet 5 to something near 6 feet 10, Tarkenton would still have a difficult time picking up receivers. Also, the Vikings are effective at throwing the ball to running backs. Our defense was to be a 3-4. This means that instead of the usual three linebackers covering running backs, we would have four active people in the same area. Offensively, it would be difficult for the Vikings to generate points against our defensive unit.

When Super Bowl Sunday broke, so did the sun. It had been raining in Southern California for several days, and weather reports indicated it could even be a wet Super Bowl. Although the clouds hung low toward the east and the mountains, the weather was perfect for football.

The game got off to a slow start as the first quarter of the game became no more than both teams exchanging punts. However, late in the first quarter the Vikings did something that no other team had ever accomplished. They blocked a Ray Guy punt and had the ball five yards away from the end zone.

This is a time when a defensive team either folds or goes out onto the field and changes the momentum. The Vikings were thinking about a touchdown or, at the very least, a field goal and the lead. But the defensive team started thinking turnover. One play later, because of aggressive and violent play, we caused a fumble and owned the football. From that point on, the game was all Oakland.

The first score came in the second quarter of a twenty-four yard field goal by Errol Mann. After that the Viking offense started to look like a ballet with a one-two-three-kick routine. Our running backs were eating up chunks of real estate while our receivers were finding gaping holes in the Vikes' secondary. A Stabler pass to Dave Casper put us ahead 10–0, still in the second period. Before the half ended, Pete Banaszak blasted in from one yard out and we went into the intermission with sixteen points while the Vikings were still trying to figure out how they had fumbled the ball on their only scoring chance of the half.

Things didn't change much in the second half as we still had things our way. Mann kicked another field goal, this time from forty yards out, and we built our lead to nineteen points.

I'll admit that even though the Vikings were outclassed, they showed true signs of comeback ability. When our defense seemed to slack off a bit, Tarkenton found Sammy White open for an eight yard touchdown pass. That play fired up the Vikings and they started making a game of it.

Momentum is a part of football that can change a game dramatically. Sometimes, one team will go flat while the other team grabs "Mo," and one of those easy football games can suddenly change into a life-and-death struggle. It was evident that the Vikings had caught fire and we had slipped. Our offensive team went out on the field after the Viking touchdown and looked anything but impressive. Three plays later, Ray Guy was in the game kicking the ball away.

Part of my job is to put out fires. The Vikings, as I said, were burning up, and I had to dig down for a special hit to cool everything off. Sammy White provided the exact opportunity I was looking for. Sammy was the Rookie of the Year and already an All-Pro receiver. He was great on long patterns and even better on a short one. Early in the game, I had hit him with a fair shot as he attempted to catch a little turn-in-pattern. It wasn't a good hit but Sammy knew I was there. As he was getting up, I said, "Don't come back here, boy, or you're liable to get hurt." Sammy smiled and walked back to the huddle. I knew the hit wasn't going to discourage Sammy from coming over the middle but I still tried to reach him verbally. Sometimes, a receiver or running back will take what you say to heart. They might get mad and try something foolish or they might worry about what you said. I was fairly certain that Sammy was too gutsy to get upset over mere words, so I knew that before the game was over he would come roaming into my area.

Just when everything looked as though the Vikings were going to come back, Sammy White ran a pattern over the middle without bothering to look for me. It was a delay pattern designed to clear me out by giving me a deep decoy to chase after and then bringing Sammy underneath into my area. I smelled the play and made a move backwards. Tarkenton glanced at me and thought I had taken the bait. Then he quickly started searching for White coming over the middle. That's exactly what I was looking for, too. I believe that Sammy must have thought I was going deep and the middle was open, because he came into my zone moving full speed.

In this situation I sit back and wait for the ball to be thrown. From there it's just a matter of building up a full head of steam and sticking the receiver just as the ball arrives in his hands. I admit that I actually did have several options to consider, but it comes back to my job and getting "Mo" back on our side. I realize that I might have intercepted the ball, or at least made an effort for the interception. But, then again, Sammy might have been able to make the catch and take it on in for a score.

My hit on Sammy White may well be the best ever in the history of the Super Bowl. It was one of those collisions that defensive people dream about and offensive people have nightmares over. Both Sammy and I were moving full speed and it was head-on. During the impact White's helmet flew ten yards downfield, his chin strap shot twenty feet into the air, and some lady sitting near Al Davis screamed, "Oh, my God! He lost his head!"

Sammy was on the ground moaning about his eyes while I stood over him and issued another warning about coming into my area and getting hurt. I knew that Sammy was in no condition to hear my voice but his teammates were. That type of devastating hit has a tendency to discourage other receivers and running backs from trying anything over our middle. I had just wasted Sammy White. It was a knockout, and, believe me, it slowed the Vikings down. When his teammates gathered around, I could hear Sammy ask, "Check my eyes! Are they still in my head? I can't see!"

After that hit, everything swung around. Banaszak scored again, Willie Brown intercepted a pass and returned it seventy-five yards, and the score was 32–7.

Late in the game I was surprised to see Sammy White back in the lineup. He's a great receiver and I respect him as a man and as an athlete. I was glad that Sammy was okay because I think he is a tremendous person.

The Vikings did manage to score again but it was over long before the final gun went off. The final score was 32–14, and for the first time ever, the Raiders were not only the winningest team in professional football but also "Number One."

7

RATING MY PEERS
IN THE NFL

Quite often I run into people who actually believe the athlete of twenty or thirty years ago was better than our modern-day athlete. I realize it is ridiculous to even consider any comparison between yesterday's and today's products; but some individuals will argue the point that Louis could whip Ali or Thorpe was a stronger and faster running back than Campbell. When considering these points, I take a historical look at progress. The airplane, for example, is not faster than the jet, a buckboard does not compare to an automobile, and athletic progress is most definitely part of the improving world.

Several years ago, an old-timer gave me quite a debate about the professional football teams of yesterday being able to compete against the teams of today. The old gentleman was emphatic when he stated that the Canton Bulldogs could have whipped the Oakland Raiders. "Canton," he said, "was a football team made of men and not sissys. Why, we never wore fancy equipment like face masks and helmets, and football was played more violently than it is today."

It was obvious the man had played professional football many years ago, and one look at his face confirmed his claim of never being permitted the luxury of a face mask or helmet. His nose was pushed all over his face and he had an ear where I have a mouth. But fancy equipment, I assured my friend, isn't a sign of weakness in the athlete. It simply is a mark of progress within the structure of the game. Furthermore, the athlete of today could never survive the brutal contact of today's wars without elaborate protective devices. But still, this old gentleman argued that he and his Canton Bulldogs would have whipped the Oakland Raiders.

Actually, there is no way we could prove to the old man that his Canton team of fifty years ago would get blitzed by many high school teams of today, and comparing them to even Tampa Bay on the professional level is absurd. But nonetheless, that old-timer stuck to his guns and will eventually go to his Creator believing the athlete of his day was better than our modern version. To satisfy my own curiosity I did a little research on the Ohio State teams of many years ago and compared them to the team on which I played. Of course, I could only arrive at a physical comparison and had no way of actually measuring the athletic potential, but the results of that investigation were amazing.

The first recorded instance of any OSU football activity took place in 1890. The football team was made up of fifteen men, seven of whom played rush line while the others filled the positions of quarterback, two halfbacks, two fullbacks, and even three substitutes. These football players were obviously men because their team picture indicated no fancy equipment—just slacks, jerseys, and beanies. It was all very interesting reading but offered little in the way of comparison between the heights and weights of the two athletic groups.

In 1906 Ohio State started publishing the heights and weights of the football players on the team, and it was fascinating. That year OSU had a twenty-member team which won eight and lost one. Incidentally, their only loss way back then was Michigan, too. Anyway, the smallest member on the team was 5 feet 7 and weighed 153 pounds while the biggest member stood a towering 6 feet 2 and tipped the scales at 190 pounds. The average height of that team was 5 feet 11 and the average weight came out to a little over 170 pounds. Certainly, their size was not overwhelming. In fact, I'm sure that if our 1970 OSU football team were going to play against a twenty-man squad that averaged around 170 pounds, Woody would have hid the scouting report from us out of the fear that his squad might seriously injure themselves falling down laughing. Again, I say that we have no way of determining the athletes' abilities, but a 5 foot 7 running back carrying 153 pounds isn't going to frighten me or anyone on the team. That running back would have to be damn swift or else he would be seriously injured once the beef caught up with him.

Now, the team I played on definitely had the size advantage. I'm not going to get into the size difference except to say that our running backs were forty pounds more than the biggest man on the 1906 football team. And if you want to consider big people, then our linemen were well over 260 pounds and they could move. In all, I don't believe an All-Star team of the college ranks in the year 1906 could have been within two hundred points of us if there were actually a way to play the game. So the athlete of today is the best this world has ever seen. When I play against a Lynn Swann or try to tackle an Earl Campbell, I am going against the best in the history of the game. Consider, if you can, what an Earl Campbell would do to any tackler of the early 1900s. I believe that after tackling or attempting to tackle Earl, they would have rushed out and invented equipment or else they would have started playing checkers. It's just ridiculous to compare the athlete of yesterday to the athlete of today. I am making this point because in rating the best players in the NFL, the players I go against, I am in fact, rating the best in the history of the sport. I admit that once in a while an exceptional athlete played in the NFL twenty or thirty years ago, but over all, the modern players are bigger, faster, stronger, and obviously better than any of yesterday's heroes.

In rating our modern football players, I'll begin with the quarterbacks. It is true that no one person can be responsible for a team winning or losing the game, but quarterbacks do have a dramatic control of eventual outcomes. After all, the quarterback calls most of the plays and handles the ball 90 percent of the time. More important, the quarterback's prime responsibility is moving the offensive team down the field into scoring position. Therefore, he is the number one man on the field.

The quarterback should be able to throw a football and make intelligent decisions, although there have been a few that lacked the mental capacity to become great. For now, let's just say it would help a quarterback's career if he could make intelligent decisions. That way, he can complement his physical abilities. Also, a quarterback must be fearless and display confidence and leadership qualities at all times. When the team believes in the quarterback, both the offensive and defensive units function better.

A good example of poor leadership by a quarterback happened with the Oakland Raiders during the early part of my professional career. Our quarterback was Daryle Lamonica. Although we won most of our games, and Daryle was given a lot of favorable ink in the newspapers, he actually hurt the Raider organization. There was much derogatory talk throughout the NFL about Lamonica being a coward, and he never did anything to dispel the rumors. It was said that all you had to do to beat the Raiders was smack Lamonica in the head, and many defensive linemen spent their Sunday afternoons with that as their objective. As I said earlier, no one person can be responsible for a team winning or losing the game, but quarterbacks do have a dramatic control of eventual outcomes. The truth was that Lamonica was gun-shy and in those physical games he was ineffective. Daryle did not possess confidence and leadership qualities and his weaknesses reflected on the whole structure of the team. We lost a game to Cleveland 7–3. During that game, the defensive team was spectacular, but Lamonica, after getting roughed up a little, failed to move the offense. When a situation of that type occurs, the defensive unit has a tendency to let down. Under Lamonica's guidance the Raiders could never have made it to the Super Bowl Championship because he disintegrated under pressure. So when you analyze a quarterback, there are many things to be considered other than just how many touchdown passes he throws.

I guess the name of Joe Namath is synonymous with

quarterbacking, and Joe offered the game many exciting moments. Joe was a fan's type of quarterback, a team man, and the type of guy the defense wanted to throw the ball. Joe had confidence, leadership qualities, and no one can ever doubt his courage; but I'd rather play against a Namath than a Stabler or Greise. Contrary to popular belief, Namath did not do a good job of reading the defensive coverages. Joe had a tendency to force the ball into the strength of a defense instead of looking for their weakness. When this happens, the end results are sometimes interceptions. Although Joe set a season passing record of more than 4,000 yards, he still was less than a 50 percent completion passer and was always near the highest in interceptions thrown. I've played against Namath, and sometimes his decisions defied all logic. Joe had the ability to set up quickly despite his bad knees and he had a quick strong release. But still, the man would force his passes into the teeth of a defensive team instead of looking for a secondary target. Maybe part of this was because of his bad knees and his inability to move around, but it was a bad habit for any quarterback to develop. In spite of everything Joe did for the game of football, I would only rate him, at best, a fair quarterback.

If someone were to write down a formula of all the basics necessary to be a great quarterback from strictly an athletic point of view, the results would read Bert Jones of the Baltimore Colts. However, if Bert Jones played for the Oakland Raiders, I'd probably spit on him. Bert might have everything a quarterback should physically and mentally have, but in my opinion he is only a little boy in a man's body. Bert, unfortunately, never grew up, and professional football is a mature game. One of the NFL rules concerns the very subject of maturity. A high school athlete cannot play in the NFL until he has sat out for five years or until his high school peers have graduated from college. This was done to protect young players who are blessed with athletic talent but still lack physical and mental maturity. Even though Bert spent his time in college and has physically matured into manhood, he shouldn't be permitted to play in the NFL because of his childish fantasies.

Bert Jones has a great arm and that ability to search out the open man. If all others fail, Bert still has enough to take off and run the ball, but professional football and quarterbacking require much more than all those abilities. Bert Jones is the type of guy who wants to be out of the locker room first and he expects the people around him to bow whenever he passes through. Bert is the kind of man who will scream and cuss at a receiver because the man dropped the ball and he will kick the ground, slap his helmet, or cry when he has overthrown a receiver. Bert needs to learn that everyone who plays football is a human first. Receivers don't want to drop passes and quarterbacks don't want to miss wide-open targets. But somewhere along the line, Bert has developed the attitude that receivers should be perfect. If I was a receiver and Bert threw a pass that I dropped, and he screamed at me with fifty thousand people in the stands and several million at home watching on the tube, I would show the fans some real action. No one, not a quarterback, a coach, nor an owner of a team, has the right to subject a player to such embarrassment. In spite of all Bert Jones's abilities, Namath was a much better quarterback than young Mr. Jones can ever hope to be.

I think that a perfect quarterback would have Kenny Stabler's mind inside Terry Bradshaw's body. I'm not taking a slap at Bradshaw's mental capacity; it's just a fact that Stabler is a physical wreck. I admit, in a way, that I am also trying to say that Ken is a much better thinker than Bradshaw. While Bradshaw can succeed with overpowering physical abilities and the daring to make things happen, Stabler is a give-and-take type of quarterback. Both men have the ability to produce the big play even though their styles differ, but for my money, I would feel better with Ken Stabler handling the ball in a pressure situation. Stabler is the type of quarterback who will look the situation over and remain cool through the heat. Bradshaw will make up his mind too quickly and sometimes be forced into mistakes. If I had written this book two years ago,

Bradshaw would have received a lower rating than Jones, but Terry's leadership qualities have surfaced recently and I do believe the man is fast becoming one of the better quarterbacks in the NFL. But when I consider my reputation as a hitter and not an interceptor, the fact that I have only intercepted twenty-six passes during my career, and seven or eight of those interceptions have been gifts from Bradshaw, does indicate a major weakness in Terry's style. He has a tendency to rattle quickly and impulsively throw the ball up for grabs, or worse yet, take off running without any regard for his safety. But like I said, the man is trying and he is improving. Who knows, if Bradshaw can keep his body together and play for another twenty years, he may well become the greatest quarterback in the history of the game. But for now, Kenny Stabler is still my number one man in the NFL.

I know that many fans are going to look at the Raiders' record last season and ask me to explain a nine and seven record and Stabler's thirty interceptions. First of all, eleven of Ken's interceptions were the results of pop-ups. Kenny threw perfect passes that hit the receivers in the hands or shoulder pads and simply popped up into the waiting arms of defenders. You don't fault the quarterback or the receiver for that kind of interception or incompletion. Those are just the breaks of the game. Also, the Raiders had a lot of new personnel on the offensive line, while at the same time, veterans Gene Upshaw and Art Shell are getting a little older and were not as effective in supplying pass protection as they had been in the past. Defensively, the Raiders also made numerous changes, and all of these different elements affected the entire season. Regardless of wins, losses, or interceptions, Kenny Stabler is the best quarterback in the NFL. Stabler is the type of man who will take whatever the defense is willing to give. If we are moving by running the ball, then he will stay on the ground. If our rushing game is ineffective, then he will go up top. Even when passing, Stabler is still going to take whatever you are willing to give. If you double cover our outside people, then he will look for the tight end. If you're playing a tough zone and the receivers are covered, he will start sending a running back into the pattern. Stabler lacks the physical status of some of the other quarterbacks in the league, but he has the experience and leadership qualities to gain my vote as the best in the NFL. Maybe next year Bradshaw will gain more composure and learn how to take whatever the defense is giving. If and when that happens, I would have to honestly say that Bradshaw is number one. But for now, it's still Kenny Stabler.

Receivers are a different breed of athletes. They must have speed and grace yet be strong and durable. They must maintain the quality of concentration and ability to catch the ball when they are under tremendous pressure. I have found receivers to be the biggest con artists in football, but it's all part of their job. They bolt off the line and give the defender a thousand false moves while trying to do something for real that will gain them that liberated step. In rating receivers, I look inside the man. Courage will make a mediocre receiver great in my estimation. Howard Twilley of the Miami Dolphins lasted many years in this league even though the experts would say he wasn't going to make it. Howard wasn't big, he wasn't fast, and he had only adequate hands. But Howard had the biggest heart I have ever seen. We played a game in Miami and I spent a miserably frustrating afternoon trying to convince Howard that it hurt to run patterns over the middle. He was good at running a short pattern over the middle, and Miami was picking up the yardage on that particular play.

I hit Howard with a few good shots, and on one occasion, he was assisted from the field. But every time I looked around, Howard was back in the game courageously running his short patterns. When a receiver cannot be intimidated, he will be effective against any type of coverage or any of the assassins in the league. Howard was paid to catch the football whether in traffic or on the open field. Even though the so-called experts in the game never rated Howard very highly, I did. He never had the natural ability to become a great receiver but he had the courage to be very effective.

There are good receivers in the league and several who border on greatness. But because a receiver's job is basically suicidal, it becomes very difficult to find the individual who will go out and play the game without being intimidated. I don't know what made Howard Twilley run but I know he was special. If all receivers played the game with his style, my job would be frightening, frustrating, and virtually impossible. Fortunately for me, most receivers can be intimidated, and that gives me the edge.

In rating the receivers whom I have played against, several do stand out. Intelligence plays an important part in a receiver's effectiveness. The receiver knows that he must catch the ball, and he understands that the ball will attract some undesirable people. The secret is to be smart enough to run a safe pattern, make the catch, and then start worrying about defensive backs trying to stick their headgears through your rib cage. Fred Biletnikoff is a fantastic receiver. Fred never had the blazing speed to go long, but he was deceptively quick on his patterns. Also, Fred was highly intelligent and never overstepped the physical limits of his body. Fred had little or no fear on patterns across the middle but was intelligent and experienced enough to pick his spots. Most of the time he would curl into the middle rather than run a reckless full-speed pattern into the teeth of the defensive unit. Above all, Fred's first concern was to catch the ball and then worry about the defenders. One bad habit many receivers get into is looking for defenders and not fully concentrating on the ball. Believe me, even if you're looking for the defensive man and you're lucky enough to see him coming, it's still going to be too late to react to anything except the hit. Most of the time, under these conditions, the receiver is going to drop the ball. Why pay the price of getting blasted if you're going to miss the pass? Biletnikoff always caught the ball and then started taking the necessary steps to protect his body. On my personal list of great receivers, Fred ranks as third.

My number one man is Paul Warfield. Paul had the speed, quickness, and ability to catch the ball under any conditions. He was a big play man and could do more than any receiver in the game. I only saw Warfield look at the defender one time before he caught the ball, while other times he was simply fearless in that way. I think Paul Warfield was a physical copy of Lynn Swann, but he had more courage. Warfield, in my estimation, is most definitely number one on my list of all-time great receivers.

When I think about the best receiver in the NFL, I consider all the aspects of the game. Twilley had the courage but lacked the speed and quickness, while Warfield had all the natural abilities but lacked blazing speed. Warfield had very good speed and was quick, but blazing speed is faster than quick. Warfield, I am told, ran the hundred in 9:7, an exceptionally fast time, but blazing speed is much faster. Speed defies coverage. It makes sense that if the wide receiver is faster than the defenders, he is usually going to be open. Blazing speed requires double coverage and special assignments, and Cliff Branch of the Oakland Raiders possesses that ability. Cliff has run the hundred in 9:2 and looked as though he was coasting. Once Cliff gets a step on the defender, the gap quickly widens to ten yards and Cliff is on his way to six points. But Cliff has more than blazing speed. When you consider the everyday basics of catching the football, running sharp patterns, and having courage plus intelligence, Cliff is overwhelming. He runs a smart pattern over the middle while concentrating on the ball. After making the catch, he has the ability to quickly spot the defenders and avoid those serious head-on shots that cripple receivers. Most important, Cliff is dangerous from any spot on the field. He has the ability to turn a five yard reception into a ninety yard gain. The Raiders have a very effective passing game because Cliff Branch requires double coverage all the time. When a receiver can beat the double coverage either short or long, the man is great. Cliff is not a record setter, only a steady All-Pro who can beat you in many ways, In 1976 he made forty-six catches for 1,111 yards. That's a little better than twenty-four yards per catch. When you consider that an offensive team only needs to pick up ten yards for a first down, it's no wonder that the Raiders are usually one of the highest scoring teams in professional football.

I realize that some people might think I overlooked Lynn Swann for personal reasons. After all, he did write some nasty letters to Pete Rozelle in my behalf and has sounded off to the press about my tackling style. But Lynn Swann has not been overlooked. I believe that Lynn is truly a superb athlete. He is graceful, has quickness and speed, and he can catch the ball like few, if any, other receivers can. Lynn Swann could be the best if it were not for his one major weakness. There have been several times when I sincerely believe that Swann has been intimidated. Sure, he has played some great games, unbelievably great games, but I have often been on the field when Lynn has actually quit. His concussion during the 1976 game at Oakland was questionable. I know that he went to the hospital, but I remember seeing him running up and down on the sidelines atfer Atkinson had blasted him. He seemed okay to me then, but when I got Stallworth, and Lynn Swann was asked to go back into the game, he suddenly fainted on the sideline. Maybe he was actually injured; I really don't know. It's just hard for me to believe that George's "semi-Hook" was that devastating. I've watched the films of that action and in my estimation the hit did not look that awesome. Quite frankly, since that incident, Lynn Swann has continually been ineffective against the Raiders. In fact, one hardly realizes he is in the game with us. I know most teams take special precautions when defensing the Steelers wide receivers but we don't. If Lynn Swann was truly a great receiver, we would be extremely cautious when playing against him. Instead, we concentrate more on Stallworth and Cunningham because they have a tendency to stick their noses into the action, whereas Lynn will not.

I give Swann all the credit in the world and sincerely understand that self-preservation is a very important part of football. Maybe if I were the receiver and he The Assassin, my reasoning would be the same as his. Maybe! But at the same time, I rather doubt it. You see, I realize that football is a contact sport and people must get hit. I'm sure Lynn Swann also realizes this, but at the same time, he is trying to play the game without actually getting involved in the serious contact. Lynn will probably continue to hide from the contact and survive playing in the NFL for many years to come. He will play many more great games and pile up his statistics against the passive teams, but he will cause little concern for the physical teams.

The tight ends are a cross between the wide receivers and a runaway freight train. Most of the tight ends have the speed to beat you on long pass patterns and the physical makeup to run through the most aggressive tacklers. Tight ends start at about 6 feet 4 inches and weigh upwards of 240 pounds. They block, catch passes, and run safeties over. Every team in the NFL has a big tight end, but the three that stand out in my mind are Dave Casper, Raymond Chester, and Russ Francis. Casper and Chester are Oakland Raiders. I am glad of that. But Russ Francis plays for New England. Russ Francis is the best tight end in football. That happens to be my opinion, and it also just happens to be almost everyone's opinion. Even the so-called experts, if you can believe they are actually right for once, agree that Russ Francis is the number one tight end. Russ Francis has the size and speed to kill you; he has intelligence, and he can catch the ball. I can believe that quarterbacks love to see a target that size running down the field. It certainly makes their job easier.

If there wasn't a Russ Francis in the league, then Dave Casper would be the number one tight end. Dave and Russ are similar in size, but Russ has a tremendous edge in speed. But what more can a tight end do than what Dave Casper does every game? He blocks the biggest linemen, flattens linebackers, catches clutch touchdown passes, runs over free safeties, and has the courage of a lion. Again, Casper could be the best, but Russ Francis can do it all, and in addition, Francis has far more speed.

Raymond Chester is another great tight end. During the 1977 play-off game with the Baltimore Colts, Raymond Chester could have been the difference in winning or losing, but the Raiders won and Raymond's team lost. That year Raymond wore a Baltimore uniform and was the tight end for the Colts. I'm not sure of the reason, but he and Bert Jones never got along. Anyway, because of their mutual disregard, Raymond was wide open on several plays but Bert wouldn't throw the ball to him. After all, if you're not going to bend down and kiss Bert's feet, then he isn't going to throw you any touchdown passes. Throughout the entire game, Bert ignored Raymond, and we won the game by six points in overtime. From his seat in the press box, Al Davis decided he needed another tight end and Raymond Chester was the man. As I said before, nearly every team in the NFL has a big tight end, but the Raiders are more fortunate than most teams; we have two of the great ones in our lineup.

Receivers are my favorite people, and next to them I like running backs. Receivers and running backs provide me with more thrills and more action than anyone else on the offensive team. On nearly every play, I have to go against a receiver in one way or another, and every so often a running back will break our first line of defense and I introduce myself to the man. There were times when the man introduced himself to me, so to speak, and those were shocking experiences. Larry Csonka, of the Dolphins wasn't what you would call a great running back but he certainly earned the respect of every defensive back in the league. Larry was the type of guy who would go out of his way to try to run you over. His size, adequate speed, and bull-like charge were more than most defensive backs wanted.

You learn early in your career that a big man will run you into the ground if you try to make a high tackle. Larry Csonka is a big man. I would venture a guess that with equipment and all, Larry Csonka probably played at 260 pounds. That is a big man and, like I said, you don't try to tackle him high. Early in my career I mistakenly jumped on big men, who carried me down the field like I was a sack of flour. After a few incidents like that, I learned to hit the big man at the angles and drive through him. But Larry Csonka was a different type of big man. Larry ran low to the ground and used his elbows to ward off tacklers. It was practically impossible to get a good solid hit on him.

I can truthfully say that he was the only man who repeatedly stung me with his abusive running style, and worse, I was never able to sting him. Larry Csonka was a very effective running back with the Miami Dolphins because of their personnel and particular style of football. The Dolphins had a good line, and they had two other excellent backs in Jim Kiick and "Mercury" Morris. During their reign, they were able to control the tempo of the game. In this type of offense, Csonka was, as I said, very effective. However, if he had played on a team that didn't have excellent offensive personnel to complement Larry's style, he naturally would have lost some of his effectiveness. Csonka was a good back, but not a great one. In looking for that special quality that makes a running back great, I would have to look at his overall contribution to the team and try to determine whether or not he has game-breaking abilities. Csonka was quite effective with a very good team, but would have had great difficulty running the ball had he played for Buffalo. O. J. Simpson, on the other hand, had the ability to make even the weakest team a serious offensive threat. When O. J. played for Buffalo, one did not beat the Bills' offensive team; they simply scored forty or fifty points on the defensive team. O. J. Simpson had the ability to make the Buffalo offense go. Regardless of their record, the Bills did score points. With a Larry Csonka in the backfield instead of the Juice, the Bills' offensive production would have been seriously impaired. O. J. had the ability, and I do say "had," to break a game open from any point on the field. He had exceptional speed, balance, and power. Several years ago O. J. was the number one running back in the league, but not any more. Time and injuries have a way of catching up with the swiftest of running backs, and then there is the ever-present reality of the ultramodern athlete, Earl Campbell.

I would advise those of you who have never tried to tackle an Earl Campbell to be careful should the opportunity arise. Actually, I have always believed in seizing opportunity and I used to look forward to meeting Earl on the field of battle. Now, I believe it is sometimes better to surround opportunity rather than try to seize it. Earl Campbell has the size of a Csonka but more drive and power in the legs—if that's possible. Also, Earl has as much balance and speed as O. J. Simpson. He can be overpoweringly abusive or he can be very elusive. Earl was only a rookie in 1978 and he hasn't fully developed mentally or physically. I think Earl will get stronger as his career develops and he will learn the little intricate techniques of being a great running back. First, he will learn that being abusive is good, but one must first hold onto the ball. I don't care how big the running back is or how fast he can run; he will not score a single point without the football. Earl Campbell has a tendency to give up the football, and that can be very costly. In 1978 we played Houston and were in serious trouble. The Oilers were winning by six points and threatening to score another touchdown: They had the ball first down and goal to go on the three yard line. On the very next play, Campbell took the ball and tried the left side of the Raiders' line. He wasn't protecting the ball, and someone knocked it loose. Ten seconds later our strong safety, Charles Phillips, was standing in the other end zone with the ball and six points on our side of the scoreboard. That ninety-seven yard fumble recovery was eventually the difference in the game, and we won.

I guess what I am trying to say is that if Earl Campbell stays healthy and learns something new every day of his career, he will go on to become the number one running back in the NFL. But the man must first learn that all the size, power, and speed isn't worth very much unless he remembers to take the ball.

For now, I believe the number one running back in the NFL is Walter Payton. Walter isn't what you would call a big running back because he's only slightly over the 200-pound mark, but he runs with big-man authority. The first time I hit Walter head-on I received a jolt. Usually, when I zero in on a ball carrier and I get him with a good straight-on shot, the man is going to fall backwards. My first experience with Payton resulted in a stalemate as we both toppled over sideways. I just couldn't believe that he ran with that much power, because he didn't have the overwhelming size. But after tackling the man a few times, I realized that he was a strong and powerful running back. Payton has the power to beat you for hard-to-get yardage up the middle and has the speed to score from any point on the field. I think he is stronger than O. J. Simpson and a more daring type of runner. For the most part, O. J. would try to finesse a defender first, and only if that didn't work would he attempt to power you. Payton is a straight-ahead type of guy who can literally explode through would-be tacklers by lowering his head and ramming straight on. Payton also has great speed, and once he gets a step on the defender, it's just God and green grass between him and a touchdown. Walter Payton does have all the physical abilities that make for a great running back, but the difference between him and the other gifted athletes laying claim to number one status is simply courage. Where Payton is a small man with a big heart, some of the other running backs in the league are big men with small hearts.

Chuck Foreman of the Minnesota Vikings is another great back who can do anything. I rate Foreman very high because of his daring and overall ability. He isn't a Walter Payton, but Foreman is a great back who makes the most of his ability. I can respect that in any athlete. Foreman doesn't have the power of a Payton or the speed of a Simpson, but he makes things happen. He has good size and plays an intelligent game. A running back like Foreman makes my position all the more challenging because I know he is a quality athlete with that blend of courage.

Whenever I think about the most gifted athlete in the NFL, Franco Harris's name comes to mind. Franco is a big back with great power and breakaway speed. But I have never seen a more imposing physical specimen of an athlete with less drive than Franco. I am aware of Franco's achievements in professional football, and they are fantastic. But at the same time, I cannot help thinking what records he could have set had Franco Harris played football with heart. Many football fans will disagree with my remarks about Franco, and I realize the impact of these statements. But to prove my judgment, I ask all football fans, even Steeler fans, to objectively observe Franco Harris in any football game. If Franco doesn't run for the sidelines, slip and fall, or cake out before anyone gets near him, then believe me, someone else is wearing his game jersey.

In 1974 we played the Steelers in Pittsburgh, and that was the first time I realized Franco wasn't an overpowering running back. The Steelers had the ball on our four yard line with a first down and goal. At that time it was a close game; I think we were ahead 7–0. In this situation, I felt certain they would give the ball to Franco on some straight-ahead play. Well, Franco got the ball and his offensive line opened a big hole. All Franco had to do was lower his shoulder and bull ahead over the Raiders' free safety for six points. In other words, all Franco had to do was run me over and he would have scored. But instead of running like a man who weighed 235 pounds against a man weighing 205, Franco ran like a real chump and I buried him. I saw Mike Webster, the Steelers' All-Pro center, look at Franco in shock. Mike was trying to figure out what had happened. The Steelers ran that same play again and again I creamed Franco with a one-on-one tackle. It was like running into soft butter, and Franco went down again. By this time, I started thinking that either I was the most vicious tackler in the universe or Franco was holding back. After a third attempt and a third burial, the Steelers gave up on Franco and tried another back in another direction. I know that Mike Webster tried to figure out what happened, and maybe now he really knows the truth. I am a pretty fair tackler, but any old lady in the stands could have run the ball in that situation and shown more class than Franco.

Since I mentioned Mike Webster, the All-Pro center for the Steelers, I may as well get into the great linemen in the game of football. The linemen are rarely mentioned and seldom given credit for their tremendous contribution to the game. Take the center, for example, Here is a man who snaps every ball back to the quarterback and then opens holes for the running backs or protects the passers. If I had a football team, I would want Mike Webster to be my center. Mike has the size, intelligence, and raw strength to ward off any defensive lineman in the league. Mike's only problem is that he plays for Pittsburgh; and if a center is going to get pushed out of the limelight on any team, it will be Pittsburgh. With the great personnel on the Steelers, it's a wonder anyone knows that Mike Webster is alive. But I'm sure the people who play against him know that he is for real.

When anyone mentions great linemen, the names of Art Shell and Gene Upshaw become synonymous with excellent line play. For many years now the Oakland Raiders have had an All-Pro line with Art, Gene, and Dave Casper at tight end. I think that Art and Gene are two very good reasons why the Raiders have an effective passing game. Whenever a quarterback is given three seconds to throw the football, the results are going to be good. But when a quarterback is given five, six, seven, or more seconds to throw the ball, the results are going to be overwhelming. As a quarterback, Ken Stabler can tell you that Gene and Art are in a league all their own.

I believe that O. J. Simpson's record breaking 2,003 yards in a season was made possible by two excellent guards. Joe DeLameilleure and Reggie McKenzie. They had the ability to open holes up front and the speed to get outside. A successful running game depends on intelligent and quick guards. I think that Larry Little of Miami is also that type of guard. When you look into any great rushing team, you will find some great individuals on the line. During Miami's reign, Larry Little was instrumental in keeping defensive people away from Dolphin running backs.

In rating the defensive people, I like to start with the middle linebackers. Actually, the middle linebacker is really the quarterback of the defensive team. He is the man who makes things happen. He calls the defensive signals and is responsible for keeping the defenders in an aggressive frame of mind. Although the middle linebacker could, as Dr. Arnold Mandall said in his book, *Nightmare Season,* "be the class president," he can also be a Jack the Ripper. The middle linebackers are most unusual characters.

I believe the best middle linebacker in the history of

the game was Willie Lanier. Willie had tremendous intelligence, a nose for the ball, was great on pass coverage, and he could hit. When you consider his size, speed, and the number of years he played in the league, you come to realize why the man was, and still is, great. I have learned something new every year in the NFL. I realize that maybe I have slowed down a little, but my experience is invaluable. Well, Willie Lanier played more than ten years, and he knew the game inside and out. Just when the offensive team figured they had Willie out of position, he would show up on the spot with an animal-like hit on some unsuspecting running back or jump up and make an interception.

Now Bill Bergey of the Eagles is the best middle linebacker in the game. Bill has everything it takes to fill that position, and he could play for any team in the NFL. There isn't a better middle linebacker in the business. However, if Willie Lanier decided to play another season, I think he would still be number one.

Steeler fans are no doubt asking about Jack Lambert. Well, Jack Lambert is a fair linebacker, but he certainly isn't in the same company with a Lanier or Bergey. Lambert is great because he plays for Pittsburgh and they have the best defensive line in professional football. With the talent Pittsburgh has on their front line, they hardly need a linebacker at all. In fact, Franco Harris could play that position and look good. Lambert is fair on pass coverage but is quite weak against the running game if a team can semi-handle the front four. In 1976 during the championship game against the Steelers, we felt our offensive line could neutralize their front four. That way, our tight end, Dave Casper, would be free to block down on Lambert. I don't have to say that Lambert was ineffective, because the score, 24–7 in favor of the Raiders, gives a good indication of the quality of Lambert's performance. Also, Lambert has trouble against teams that can get a running back through the front four on any type of straight-ahead play. If all the running backs in the league were sideline-to-sideline Francos, then Lambert would look good all the time. But, unfortunately, some running backs actually do run straight ahead, and once in a while, they even get past the Steelers' front four. Then, I'm sorry to say, Lambert is usually quite useless.

So that Steeler fans will not get the idea that I don't respect any of the men wearing the gold and black, let me give my opinion about their outside linebacker, Jack Ham. Jack Ham is truly a great professional. He has the ability to do everything an outside linebacker should do and much more. Ham can tackle, cover the pass, and find the ball in any situation. Again, Ham, like Lambert, is playing behind the greatest defensive line in the game, but I sincerely believe that Jack Ham could play great football with the Giants, Jets, or the Pottstown Firebirds; whereas Lambert would only be effective with the Steelers.

Another great linebacker is Randy Gradishar. When Denver drafted Randy, they drafted a perennial All-Pro. Gradishar is just a shade below Jack Ham and Bergey. He's one of those players who seem to be completely out of the play until you look around to see who made the tackle or the interception. I have watched him play for the last several years, and he is amazing. His range and movements are fantastic.

Considering the defensive line and the great ones in those positions, I simply think of the Pittsburgh Steelers of 1975. I don't think any team in the history of football has had four more talented athletes playing on the defensive line than Pittsburgh. I'll even go as far as to say that I doubt whether any team in the future will ever have a better defensive line than the Pittsburgh Steelers. I know that might sound like a contradiction, but let me explain. During the glory years of the Steelers, and they are still actually enjoying those years, Chuck Noll assembled the greatest defensive line in football. What happened was that Pittsburgh ended up with an All-Pro defensive line in the likes of L. C. Greenwood, Ernie Holmes, Joe Greene, and Dwight White. They were simply awesome. I realize that athletes will continue to improve, so the younger members of Pittsburgh's front four will improve as the older ones decline, but it will take some doing to again place four such athletes on the same team on the field at the same time. The Steelers did it in 1975, and I doubt if it can ever be repeated.

Another great defensive lineman worth mentioning is Louis Kelcher of San Diego. Louie looks like a refrigerator; one of those twenty-five-cubic-feet ones. Louie is big. I don't mean just big in a tall sense; I mean big all over. The first time I saw him all I could think of was a refrigerator. At first, I didn't think that anyone built like a refrigerator could move well enough to play football, but when he started flattening our people, everyone began asking, "What the hell was that?" Then you would hear the San Diego fans start chanting "Looou, Loooou, Looooou." It was frightening, and "Looooou" went crazy knocking the hell out of everyone.

There are many excellent defensive linebackers and linemen in the NFL, but I have just mentioned a few of the ones who come to mind; the ones I consider far above average. Now, that leaves only the defensive backs to rate.

Anytime I hear the term "defensive back," I immediately think of our cornerback, Willie Brown. I guess that's because I first heard about Willie when I was playing high school football, and then again when I played in college, and ever since I've played in the NFL. Willie admits to thirty-eight or thirty-nine years, but sometimes I think he's much older. That's when I see him walking around town slowly or telling some young receiver to take it easy on him. Then, there are times when Willie swings into action and I think he is younger than he admits to being. Willie is one of those remarkable athletes who time seems to forget about, or at least it passes a little slower for them. Willie is remarkable because he is always expected to retire and yet comes out for the team every year and contributes. I think that now it has become a matter of experience rather than quickness, but still Willie Brown can stay with the youngest and quickest receivers. Not only that, in Super Bowl XI, Willie picked off a Fran Tarkenton pass and returned it seventy-five yards for a touchdown. In my estimation, Willie is one of the real experts at cornerback.

Other experts include Mel Blount of Pittsburgh and Mike Haynes of New England. Both these defenders are a rare cross between a push-and-shove, man-for-man defender and a slashing assassin in their zone. Both are excellent at pass coverage and both possess knock-out power in tackling.

I guess my rating system should also include coaches. Actually, a fielded football team is nothing more than an extension of its coach. If a coach is passive, his team will reflect that style; if the coach is aggressive, his team will be aggressive, too. Coaches do not go out and battle on the field like the players, but they are part of the war and part of the system. For coaches and players alike, the system is simply to produce or you're gone.

George Allen is a well-traveled coach. Several years ago he left the Rams for Washington. Later he left Washington for the Rams, and then he left football for good. Actually, he was booted out of football because he didn't produce. Allen's theory was that you win with old vets who have the experience. Now I admit that experience is a very important part of football, but so are youth and new blood. When I was in college, I had the ability to run forty yards in 4.3 seconds. But as my experience increased, so did my time in running the forty yard dash. Experience, I'm afraid to say, is a luxury enjoyed only by the older football players. Time is the price one pays to gain experience, and with age one will lose that quickness and speed of his daring youth. George Allen failed to realize that and developed his teams around football's old-timers. To a degree, experience can be a tremendous asset, but over the long run the old man is going to wear down, and all the experience in the world isn't going to pay off if he's falling down wheezing and gasping for a breath of air. Experience will push you, but the old body won't carry you to the point of accomplishment. While Allen was with the Rams, he had some excellent players with the needed experience. But again, he lacked the new blood. In Washington, George Allen again gave up his draft picks for veterans and almost won football games. When he made his triumphant return to Los Angeles, he followed the same pattern—trade the draft choices for experience and almost win.

Coaches have their individual styles, and they all differ. Some of them stand out in a crowd, and so do their teams, while others seem to fade into a background of colorless expression and neither suffer much nor enjoy much. Who's the coach for the Saints, Atlanta, the Redskins, the Giants, or just about any of eighteen or nineteen teams that lack the luster of championship form? What I'm trying to say is that most football fans can only associate with a winner. Talk about football teams and the average fan will start with Pittsburgh and Noll or Landry and Dallas, and move on to names like Lombardi, Madden, Brown, and Ewbank. Winning is the only thing that counts, whether you're a player, a coach, or the water boy. And I believe it all starts with the man at the controls—the head coach. A perfect coach is one who doesn't disintegrate under pressure and has the intelligence to look into tomorrow. He must also be fair, have compassion and understanding for his players, and burn with the desire to win.

I'm going to start out by talking about my ex-coach, John Madden. John was forced into retirement by ulcers and nothing else. I know the rumor had it that John was asked to step down because of the bleak 9 and 7 season the Raiders went through in 1978, but that's not true. For health reasons alone, John was unable to continue coaching. Believe me, if he had been fired, and the health factor hadn't been the sole reason for his early retirement, John would have accepted a job at any one of the six or seven teams that called him. But the pressures of the battle and that consistent grind to win finally caught up with the man, and he has gone back into a more serene life of simply being a fan.

When I look at the man, John Madden, I see something special. He could deal with people on any level, and the Raiders' success and development of their personnel offer proof of that statement. Look down our roster to see what I mean. Many of the Raiders were a band of misfits, rogues, and ruffians who couldn't get along with their own mothers until Madden took over.

Some of our guys have been in more football camps than they can remember, and because of their attitudes, were branded as undesirables. But Madden had a way of taking the undesirables and turning them into a functioning machine that gave him the highest winning percentage of all the coaches in the NFL. There have been coaches who have won more total games than John but none have attained a win-loss ratio as impressive as his.

A coach has to be able to understand his players. John had the ability to communicate with anyone on the team, even Skip Thomas. I don't mean to slight Skip. It's just that Skip had different ideas, but John was able to understand and love the man. Skip is a tremendous athlete, but most teams would have given up on him a long time ago. John took everything in stride, though at times it was tough. For example, we were once in Houston getting ready for an important game and John received a phone call about Skip. At that time, Skip was on the injured list and in a hospital in Los Angeles. This hospital administrator was cussing out John because Skip brought his motorcycle into his hospital room. Well, John pacified the administrator and then called Skip. Most guys would have gone berserk, but John calmly asked Skip what the trouble was. Skip said, "I don't want some nigger stealin' my bike!"

If you know Skip and understand about his bike and his car, you realize it was a serious problem to the man. I know it sounds crazy but Skip really cares about his bike and doesn't want anyone touching it, much less stealing it. It wouldn't be a problem for most people, but John realized what it meant to Skip. He took time from his busy schedule and made arrangements for the bike to be taken out of the hospital and put in a safe place.

What I'm trying to say is that John understood people and could talk to and get along with anyone. Because of John we had a relaxed atmosphere in our camp, but that didn't mean the conditioning and working aspects of professional football were lacking. John believed that we were men first and professional athletes second. His style of conditioning was to let us do it on our own. If we cared enough about our bodies and our jobs, then he cared, too. If we didn't care about getting into shape, that simply meant we didn't care much about our job, and from there it was a quick trip to the exit gates.

Madden knew football inside and out, and his teams reflected his personal desire to be the best coach in football. When a coach has pride and wants to win, his players will develop that same attitude.

Madden was a great coach and a great man, but there have been others in the business, too. Vince Lombardi was a forceful type of coach. He believed in a tough conditioning program and a simple play book drilled to perfection. He was a hard-working and extremely aggressive man with an appetite for winning. His players rallied around Vince and would fight to the last second of every football game. That deep-rooted relationship between players and coach developed because it all started on a man-to-man basis. Lombardi would say, "I'll treat you like a man until you prove yourself otherwise." When a coach respects his players, the players will respect their coach. Lombardi was a credit to the game, God rest his soul.

I think Chuck Noll is another great coach, and his most fantastic asset is vision. Noll has a great ability to look into the future and picture what a young athlete is going to look like years from now. I believe that while Chuck Noll is coaching right now, his vision is three or four years ahead of the present action. Noll took what was once the worst team in the history of football and made a complete turnabout. He used his draft picks wisely and also developed previously unheard of athletes into All-Pros. The Steelers are two and three deep in every position and every year they seem to land two or three more blue chippers. This is because of Noll's vision and contant planning for the future. In all his years of coaching, Chuck Noll has made only one mistake, and we need not cover the running backs again.

Coaches, as I have said, all have different styles. Don Shula, for example, is a very serious individual who seems distant to me. I don't know the man personally but from talking with some of his players, I get the feeling that Shula keeps a distinct line between the players and coaches, whereas other winning coaches try to develop a feeling of camaraderie between the players and the coaching staff. Shula is successful in his environment but I doubt that such a man could keep the Raiders under control. In my estimation, strait-laced coaches like Shula, and possibly Landry, would have a tendency to make things a little sticky. I'm not saying that they are not successful people in their jobs; it's just that they win with a different type of athlete. I personally like a coach who will jump up and down once in a while or show a little enthusiasm toward players who are doing a good job or making that great play. Landry, Shula, and Bud Grant of the Vikings always have that uncommitted expression on their faces. I don't need a coach hugging me and showering me with affection, but I like the idea of a man saying, "Well done, great play, or get 'em next time." Still, though, one cannot argue with success, and Shula, Landry, and Grant have had their special moments, and I respect that accomplishment.

There are two coaches, no longer in the game and quite opposite in style, whom I think about quite often. The first man is Weeb Ewbank and the second is Hank Stram. Ewbank is the only coach to win championships in both leagues. Weeb won a championship with the Colts and then again with the Jets in the Super Bowl of 1969 that proved to the world that the American Conference had arrived. I think Weeb was effective in his days because he had the vision to try something new. But if Ewbank were coaching today, his system would be totally ineffective. In studying Ewbank's teams, one can see a trend slanted toward the smaller, quicker type of player. Weeb believed in speed and quickness first and size second. As a result, he found the speed and quickness he desired in an athlete in men of questionable size. It wasn't so very many years ago that a professional lineman could get by if he weighed only 220 or 230 pounds. But not anymore. Because of weight and strength techniques and better diets, the professional football players have grown in both size and speed. Weeb stressed speed and quickness and seemed unaware of the fact that a good big man is going to beat the hell out of a good small man. Speed and quickness have a place in football, but so do size and strength. Successful teams have that combination of good overall quickness and speed blended with size and strength. In selecting an ideal lineman, Weeb would end up with a defensive end who could run the forty in 4.7 but had the body of a 200-pound defensive back. Other teams would go after the defensive end who ran a 4.75 forty and stood 6 feet 5 and weighed 270 pounds. Which man is going to win the battle?

In 1971 Weeb's theory built on yesterday's visions was shattered by today's realities. The small quick man was out and the bigger and increasingly quicker man was in. Weeb's New York Jets spent more time in the hospitals than they did on the playing field.

Hank Stram, however, believed in the biggest players he could find. Hank's idea was to first find the giants and then teach them to develop speed and quickness. Well, speed and quickness can be developed to a degree, but you don't take a lumbering 6 feet 10 tight end and make him capable of 4.5 speed. Stram was a great coach and a very successful man, but I feel that his teams needed a little more balance. Stram had some great players and won a Super Bowl, but I believe he could have improved by looking for a little more overall team speed and quickness. I can't help but think what a combination Ewbank and Stram would have made. Weeb would have been looking for the speed and quickness in players and Hank would have been in search of the giants. Finding the player with that blend of size and quickness would be finding an All-Pro.

I think Paul Brown was a pretty fair coach, too. He had the ability to size up ballplayers and develop weak areas on a team. But more important than all of that, Paul had that innovative flair for the unexpected. I remember playing against the Bengals early in my career, when Paul took us by surprise. We were holding on to a slim three-point lead with the time running down. The Bengals had the ball and could at best run one or two more plays. It was one of those situations that called for a pass and a prayer, but Brown sent his fullback up the middle on a draw play. It was an absurd call, but the man went seventy yards for a score.

Now, there are bums coaching professional football teams and then there is a Bum Phillips. I'm not going to get into the bums, but I am going to mention Bum Phillips and Houston. Bum Phillips looks like a reject from the rodeo, with his cowboy garb, but the man is something special to his boys. You see, Bum is the type of guy who loves his players and they love him. It's a style that some individuals can use effectively to get players to go the extra mile. At heart Bum is a winner with his own personal touch of class. The players can associate with him and by blending the talents of players and knowledge of coaching into a workable system, Bum has accomplished great things with the Houston Oilers.

Maybe some readers will feel that I have been particularly hard on their favorite superstar, but I've only tried to be open and honest. I tell it the way I see it and the way I know it happens. Actually, you don't have to play free safety for a professional team to pick up on the true character and abilities of the players around the league. Just watch any NFL game and you'll see what I mean. The great one will be great regardless of the situation, while the phonies will show their true color.

In 1978 I was watching ABC's "Monday Night Football" and Bert Jones gave one of his most unforgettable performances. Bert was coming off a serious shoulder injury and seemed to be having great difficulty throwing the ball on the sidelines. ABC had a sideline camera zeroed in on Jones and every time he lifted his arm to throw the ball, the expression of pain registered on his face. It was dramatic and touching. Howard Cosell went on and on about Bert's great courage and what a man he was to play under those painful conditions. It was so touching that I almost had tears in my eyes watching Bert's show and listening to Cosell's words of praise to the king. Bert would throw a weak and wobbly pass, grimace with pain, and let his right arm dangle loosely at his side. My, but it was touching. Then the game started and Bert struggled out on to the field with his right arm dangling as though it were broken in fifty or sixty places. What an effort! What a show!

"If only Hollywood were watching," I thought, "then Bert would surely be in the movies come tomorrow."

Everything seemed blown up to me. I've seen players with their arms pulled out of the sockets and they looked better at the time of the accident than Bert did 95 percent recovered. But it was Bert Jones and his dramatic return to professional football, so I anxiously watched.

Then it happened. With tearful eyes, the brave Mr. Jones dropped back for his first pass of the evening and uncorked an eighty yard incompletion. His arm hurt and he doubled over in pain, but still he tried again. Next he fired a bullet pass over the middle for a completion. This time his arm didn't hurt. Throw an interception or incompletion and the pain in that right shoulder was unbearable, but throw a completion and it didn't hurt? Right then, Bert received my nomination for the Academy Awards, and with that I turned off the television.

It's like I said, you don't have to play football in the NFL to begin to understand the character and courage of the people who make up the game.

I know by now everyone is asking, "What does Jack Tatum think of Jack Tatum?" and I will answer that question. First of all, my college coach was once asked in my presence, "Woody, who was the best athlete you ever coached?"

"Well," Woody answered, staring out of his window at St. John's Arena, "it wasn't Jack Tatum. Jack was one of the best, but I think Archie Griffin was the greatest ever."

Then Woody was asked, "Who was the best pass defender you ever coached?"

Woody answered, "Well, it wasn't Jack. I think maybe Tim Fox."

Then the same person asked, "Woody, who was the best hitter you ever coached?"

Woody, without a second of hesitation, said, "That was Jack Tatum! Without a doubt, Jack Tatum was the hardest hitter I ever coached or saw play the game of football. Why our own people were scared to death to go out and even practice against him."

Well, I don't think I'm exceptional when it comes to interceptions, but in a way, that really isn't my job. What's more, I never really found intercepting passes all that exciting. I believe my game is built around contact. I am paid to hit, so I hit. There are safeties in the NFL who are better than me at playing the ball, but when it comes to making a tackle, I like to believe most receivers and running backs wish I didn't exist.

8

ME, AN ASSASSIN?

After eight or nine years in the NFL, you have a tendency to start counting your stitches, bumps, and bruises and looking at a future day when your body will start to slow down a little and physical exercise will not be a necessary way of life. When that happens, I know that arthritis and bursitis will settle into my bones and joints and yesterday's hits on wide receivers will become tender and stiff areas of my body. Humans were just not built with the contact of professional football in mind. And regardless of all the conditioning a football player does, there is still the chance of serious injury and still a price that will be paid during old age. Even now, it gets more difficult for me to get out of bed for days after a game. I know that is simply a combination of the aging process and football's minor injuries catching up with me. Still, though, it's the type of work I have chosen and the price I must pay, and, hopefully, when my NFL career is over, I'll still be able to stand upright and walk like a human being.

I have really been lucky during my career. In high school I was never seriously injured. During my college days I was hit from the blind side just once; knocked senseless for a few minutes; and then I went back into action. I had only received some minor bumps and twists throughout my scholastic career. In professional football my luck has thus far continued. I've only had but a few injuries compared to some of the athletes in the NFL.

Whenever I consider my personal injuries, I only count the injuries that prevented me from playing in a game. Under game conditions I know that I will bleed and bruise. I can't remember the number of times my head or face has been stitched up during a game or afterwards, but that's to be expected in the NFL. Sometimes a finger gets past your face mask and into your eyes or a part of equipment scrapes against your body. Those are little injuries, areas of pain with which you still play the game. I even split my head open during brutal contact and still went back into the game. That type of injury requires only a towel to wipe the blood from your eyes and a few stitches to return you back to the action.

The injuries that add up and really hurt are, as I said, injuries that prevented me from playing in or finishing a game. My knee injuries have been of this type. I have twice undergone operations for knee problems. That usually requires a week or more in the hospital and six solid weeks of rehabilitation. Sometimes a person doesn't come back after knee surgery with the full range of motion he had previously. Other times the knee joint is never normal again and requires more surgery and much more time in rehabilitation. There are many players in the NFL who have had their knees operated on six, seven, and eight times. I know that Joe Namath and his four knee operations have been well publicized, but few people know that our All-Pro center, Jim Otto, has had at least ten knee operations that he can remember. At least Namath can walk without the aid of special knee braces. Jim Otto can't. Before he gets out of bed in the morning, Jim straps braces on his knees to keep them from collapsing. Jim Otto played NFL football and paid the price during his career with hard physical work and dedication to a job. But now, and for the rest of his life, Jim Otto will carry the scars of his NFL career and continue to pay for his achievements with pain. He wasn't as lucky as I.

Although I have been lucky, I still have had more injuries than just a few to the knees. One time, during a game against the Steelers, I tore all the muscles in my groin. I've also had a slight shoulder separation, neck injuries, and my hands look as though a cable car in San Francisco parked on them for a night. After my career is over, I'm going to get my hands and fingers operated on. I want my fingers to be straightened out a little to make them look at least halfway normal, and I'd like to be able to someday move all my fingers. Who knows, maybe someday I might want to learn how to play the piano or guitar.

In all, I would say that during my career I have only missed, on the average, two or three games per season. In the NFL that is a remarkable record. I know there are those who have never missed a game because of injuries, but most of those guys give less than 100 percent. For the most part, when playing in the NFL, one accepts the fact that he will be injured. Every player who goes into battle understands that at any second, on any play, his career could come to an abrupt and tragic conclusion.

August 12, 1978, I was involved in a terrible accident with Darryl Stingley, a wide receiver who played for New England. On a typical passing play, Darryl ran a rather dangerous pattern across the middle of our zone defense. It was one of those pass plays where I could not possibly have intercepted, so because of what the owners expect of me when they give me my paycheck, I automatically reacted to the situation by going for an intimidating hit. It was a fairly good hit, but nothing exceptional, and I got up and started back toward our huddle. But Darryl didn't get up and walk away from the collision. That particular play was the end of Darryl Stingley's career in the NFL. His neck was broken in two places and there was serious damage to his spinal cord. Darryl Stingley will never run a pass pattern in the NFL again, and it may well be that he will never stand up and walk across a room. For weeks Darryl lay paralyzed in a hospital and there were times when, because of complications after surgery, he nearly lost his life.

I want to be tough and I work at playing the game hard, but within the structure of the rules. Still, though, there are times when I wonder about myself and the structure of NFL football. I am tough, but I'm not a brutal animal. I think it's possible for a football player

to be proficient in his job and still possess sentiment.
I want to do my job, and the contact of the sport doesn't
bother me, but I certainly don't want to hospitalize
Lynn Swann and I wasn't thinking about killing Riley
Odoms.

When the reality of Stingley's injury hit me with its
full impact, I was shattered. To think that my tackle
broke another man's neck and killed his future . . . well,
I know it hurts Darryl, but it hurts me, too.

One week later we had an exhibition game against
the Rams. The Stingley incident was still troubling me.
I didn't know if I wanted to play in the game against
the Rams. In fact, I didn't know if I could ever play
football again. During the week I had spent some very
trying hours talking with the doctors about Darryl's
condition. That was constantly on my mind and tearing
at my insides. My head was a ball of throbbing pain and
my body felt like a hollow shell that no longer belonged
to me. And then, too, I couldn't help but think about
negotiating for a new contract this past season and how
Al Davis had handled everything. Davis, I know, is
nothing more than a company man, and if you wanted
to play for nothing, and the NFL accepted that contract, it would be fine with Al. If you want a million
dollars for three years, Al will try to get you a hundred
thousand. I don't fault the man for doing his job, but
he does make it difficult for an athlete when it comes
time to talk about new contracts.

In 1977 I had played out my option and was looking
for more money with the next contract. To be perfectly
honest, I did have some loyalty to the Oakland Raiders,
but I couldn't pay my bills and completely establish myself for the future with that loyalty. I wanted money . . .
more money.

Al Davis started our contract talks by trying to cut
my pay. When it came time to explain his reasons, he
had thousands, and if I had given him the time, I'm sure
Al would have come up with a million reasons why he
wanted to cut my pay. But the crux of the matter was
that I intended to end up making more money and
whichever color uniform I put on really didn't matter.
To me, my future in the NFL was a matter of green

and nothing else. Al still cited incidents during games
when I missed a tackle or failed to knock someone out.
He started with a game several years ago when we were
beating the hell out of Cincinnati, and late in the game,
Archie Griffin got by me and scored. At the time, I was
a little tired, and lazy, too. That touchdown had no
bearing on the game but Al still thought I should have
blasted Archie. From there he verbally replayed almost
every game of my career and pointed out situations in
which I had not done the job the Oakland Raiders were
paying me to do. The whole thrust of the contract talks
with Al centered around the notion that I was not hitting like I did earlier in my career. Al Davis was telling
me that I was paid to be a war head, and anyone who
came near me should get knocked into hell. Al left me
with the impression that my only marketable talents in
professional football were those of an intimidator. My
job with the Raiders was that of a paid assassin. Well,
so be it.

Again, one expects this kind of situation whenever it
comes time for a new contract. The management will
point out your failures while you bargain from strong
points. It's only good business. But now, after the
Stingley incident, it all began to trouble me. I started
thinking that the Raiders actually did want me in their
secondary for the expressed purpose of intimidating receivers, running backs, or any opponent, as the press
had indicated.

It was a week of soul-searching. I have always believed in working hard for the things I want out of life.
In a way, I was accomplishing all my objectives, but
when the safety of another man's life is the cost for
personal or team goals, I wondered if my objectives
really meant that much to me. Yes, I want to do my job,
and that requires hitting and intimidating opponents,
but breaking someone's neck, or even worse, shouldn't
be the price anyone must pay.

I thought about our first exhibition game of the year
and how I had played. Actually, I was only in for one
quarter, but because of my hits two members of the
Chicago Bears were carried off the field. The Raiders'
front office told my attorney that I was playing the best

football of my career. That was a strange statement coming from the Raiders, because in May Al Davis had tried to convince me that I was over the hill and a pay cut was in my future. Then I go out in our first exhibition game, knock two receivers cold, and once again I'm a great ballplayer. I was wondering if the Raiders would think I was worth a million dollars because of my last performance.

It might sound wrong for me to knock the Raider organization and how they arrive at the dollar and cent value a player is worth, but in professional football a passive free safety isn't paid as much as one who has the physical ability to inflict fear and damage on opponents. The Raiders don't exactly tell me that I must knock out receivers and running backs, but everything about the game encourages hard and violent play, and the more violently I play, the more the Raiders appreciate me. My life and career sounds like a contradiction, and maybe it really is. After hitting Darryl Stingley, I started thinking about professional football and the safety of all the players, including myself. I don't want my neck broken. I don't like to think about receiving a serious injury any more than I relish the idea of being guilty of inflicting that type of suffering on someone else. But at the same time, I have a job to do, and what happens if I slack off?

I did play in the game against the Rams. I shouldn't even have dressed for it. My mind wasn't on the field and my heart was back at the hospital bed where Darryl Stingley was fighting for his life. For the first time in my career I played a game with a passive attitude, and it hurt me. It wasn't a physical pain that I received, but my pride was wounded. On what started out as a normal running play, I zeroed in on the Ram's Wendell Tyler. It was one of those head-on shots that I usually win by knocking the back into the stands, but this time it was different. I came up and met the play flat-footed and passive. I wasn't moving with any velocity and was just hoping to get hold of Tyler and bring him down. Seconds later I was flat on my back as Wendell ran me over. It was a shocking and very embarrassing situation. Even had I knocked Tyler out with one of my bone-jarring tackles, it wouldn't have proven anything. I think that now I look at professional football in a more mature way, and say there must be a happy medium and a better way of controlling the game. From my own point of view, if I sit back passively, every running back in the NFL will make tracks over my fallen body, and before long the Raiders will have a just cause to ship me out. I like the game of football, and contact doesn't scare me in the least. But at the same time, I do care very much about myself and the opponents I tackle. Football is a contact game, and we must never forget that, but there should be a line drawn somewhere to separate hard contact from animal brutality. As a free safety, I must hit hard and be intimidating, but a measure of protection can be added by simply changing the rules of the game.

Every year the NFL meets with the owners and goes into rule changes, but it amounts to a waste of time and money. In the last few years, what rules have actually been changed to ensure the safety of the players? When you consider the rule changes that have been made, they all have been designed to make the game more exciting, and believe me, excitement in professional football mans higher risks for the players. A good example of a rule change to generate more excitement has made the most dangerous play in all of professional football occur much more frequently. I'm talking, of course, about the kick-off. Several years ago the ball was kicked from the forty yard line. With strong legs, the modern kicking stars were booting the ball out of the end zone most of the time. The ball would be spotted on the twenty yard line, since the run back had been eliminated. That wasn't a terrible thing, but some ranking official in the NFL decided that the fans were being cheated out of the excitement of the kick return, so the rules committee moved the kicker back to the thirty-five yard line. Thus, you have the excitement of twenty-two bodies building up full heads of speed and slamming into each other. The very first injury I ever sustained came on the kick-off team. Returning kick-offs is dangerous, and covering kick-offs is dangerous, but because the kick-off is exciting, some whiz who sits behind a desk in an office decides to move the kicking team back five yards to ensure the kick return. If someone wants to start changing some of the rules to make the game safer, then start by putting the ball back on the forty yard line and let those strong legs boot the ball the hell out of the end zone.

It seems that few of the rule changes are channeled into the area of safety. I know that the owners of the NFL teams, the players, and the league officials often talk about how to protect the athletes, but little is ever really done to satisfy the players' complaints. I want to play football by the rules, and I don't want to see any more necks broken. When I stop and look back over my career, I can say in all honesty that cheap shots have never been part of my game plan. But at the same time, I admit to using the rules to my advantage. Sure, I could just make tackles without really trying to blast through the man, but I am expected to, and the rules are designed in my favor because people want the excitement of violent play.

The Raiders play a zone for the most part, and as I have said before, I really don't have a specific responsibility except to seek out the ball and blast into opponents. A zone coverage is dangerous for receivers and running backs who attempt any patterns over the middle. Running a pass route through a zone defense is similar to running full speed through a woods in the middle of the night. The offensive man simply cannot see the defenders like he can in a man-to-man defense. And all teams play a zone defense. The zone is designed so that linebackers and safety personnel have areas to cover, rather than people. In my position I just sit back, watch the quarterback for any indication about where he is going to throw the ball, and then, wham! A receiver is looking for, and concentrating on, the ball while running a pattern full speed across the middle, and the free safety acts like a missile homing in on the man's rib cage, head, or knees. It's got to hurt the receiver, and after a few hits, the man's will to win is warped. I wouldn't want to be a receiver. In fact, with the rules structure as it now stands, I wouldn't play football in the NFL if I was a receiver. Playing wide receiver and running patterns over the middle against any team, passive or otherwise, is the most insane thing anyone could ever do. I realize this and can truly understand why some receivers get gun shy on crossing patterns. Okay, do I let the receiver have the edge and give him the chance to make catches around me because I'm a sensitive guy or do I do what I am paid to do? The answer is obvious, and my career bears testimony to whether or not I earn my money. But nonetheless, something must be done to give the receivers a chance, and it comes back to the rules.

The owners and the NFL officials should make player safety their number one priority when it comes time for their annual meeting. It wouldn't be that difficult to change the ruling in favor of the receiver, and I would not resent it. Just outlaw zone coverages and move every team to a five-man defensive line. With man-for-man coverage, the game becomes more of a push-and-shove, bump-and-run game. When I have to cover on a man-for-man situation, I must run with, or chase after receivers. There isn't any camping in the middle of the field and looking for those head-on shots that can render a man unconscious or break his neck. The purpose of the five-man line would also be a step in the offensive team's favor. This way, most teams would probably go with two linebackers instead of three or four, but still have four safeties. Without a group of surly linebackers mopping up on short-range passes, those areas would be more vunerable to short passes. This type of rule would also give added protection to the running back and open up the offensive aspect of football tremendously.

Another valid point to consider is doing away with the dangerous quick slant. A quick-slant pattern is designed for a six or seven yard gain or an incompletion. The receiver bolts off the line and fakes to the outside, then quickly slants in toward the middle. The defender has no chance at the ball, and the quarterback will either complete the pass or it will fall incomplete. This is a risky pattern because the defensive secondary must target the receiver and forget about the ball. You must hit the receiver and forget about the fumble or at least make him wary of your presence on the next attempt.

In that now tragic game, New England was good for at least five quick slants, and we took the necessary steps to protect against that particular play. Unfortunately, Darryl Stingley paid the price with a broken neck. I remember that moment too well. Once again, for the safety of the player, they absolutely should outlaw the quick slant.

We have talked about protecting the quarterback, and believe it or not, there *are* rules designed to offer protection. It is illegal to hit a quarterback after he has thrown the ball, but many times this is a judgment call that requires all the officials to use the same judgment. Again we are back in the area of officials lacking consistency. I believe that particular rule should be enforced in favor of the quarterback even if the play is close. I'm sure if the officials started calling these plays a little closer the defensive lineman would be careful of late hits. At least I believe they would consider the possibility of a flag and fifteen yards going against the defense. But at the same time, a little balance is needed. I mean this league is filled with smart-ass quarterbacks who will take off on a fifteen yard run and then slide into second base when the defenders close in. Several years ago, Steve Grogan took off on a little boot-leg play and when I moved in for a tackle, he fell down. Because of the rules, I simply downed him and the official threw a flag. Damn it! A player isn't considered tackled and down until a defender has made contact with him. I was doing my job and still received a fifteen yarder. Another thing is the quarterback pump-faking. That is simply a quarterback ploy to slow down the defender or fake the man off his feet into the nickle stands. Let the quarterback drop back to pass or even roll out, and lets give him the protection of flagging the close calls. But, no more pump-faking and no more slides into second base. While the quarterback is in the motion of passing the ball and he gets hit, then call the play. And if the quarterback takes off and crosses the line of scrimmage then let him pay the price. This way the quarterback will be offered a little more protection from the rules, while at the same time the defenders won't feel cheated.

A new rule has been added this year that experts claim will "offer the quarterback more protection." I think the rule is a waste of time and bunk. This season, when a quarterback is in the clutches of a defender the officials will blow the play dead. I don't believe that is going to offer the quarterback any more protection and that particular rule will take away from the game. Quite often, quarterbacks have the ability to break free and complete the pass or run for extra yardage. Actually, this type of rule is putting professional football on a touch football plain. I'm all for giving the quarterback protection with the rules, but let's keep some balance within the structure. Let's not jump from one end of the spectrum to the other.

Another ruling that should be changed would offer the quarterback a little protection.

When several sports writers asked the question about special considerations for quarterbacks, Steeler linebacker Jack Lambert said, "Give 'em dresses!" Obviously, that statement was a weak attempt at humor over a serious problem. Quarterback injuries are a serious threat to the success of any team so you would think the owners would push for this change. They don't. Like Lambert, they think only of blitzing the other team's quarterback and knocking him out of the game. I wonder what Lambert thinks about when it's his own quarterback writhing in pain because he took a split second too long in releasing the ball. I've seen Bradshaw wobble to the sidelines wondering where he was after taking a shot in the head by an overzealous lineman or linebacker. Naturally, it all becomes a different situation to Mr. Lambert and the Steelers when it's their quarterback asking "Who am I?"

Quarterbacks should be protected! Quarterbacks must be protected, and I'm not talking about better-blocking linemen. I think special consideration should be given to a man who drops back in a pocket to pass the football. A quarterback can't fight back, and in a passing position I believe he is the most vulnerable to serious injury of any man on the field. A quarterback stands there looking down the field, concentrating on the type of coverage, and searching for that opening. The big defensive linemen and linebackers start coming after him at full speed and he knows he will get clobbered whether or not he gets the pass off. It takes a brave individual to still stand in there, deliver the ball, and take a hit.

Many changes in the rules can offer more protection to the quarterbacks. First of all, blitzing could be eliminated. In every All-Star or All-Pro game, there is a no-blitz ruling. This is a step at protecting the quarterback. Blitzes create weaknesses in the pass protection and usually are designed to give one defender a free route to the quarterback's head. If the people who set up the rules outlaw the blitz during All-Star games, why not exercise that same reason and sanity for the regular season? I'm not saying they should put dresses on the quarterbacks, because that was an absurd solution to a serious problem. But let's give the quarterback a special consideration. I wonder what type of courage Lambert would exhibit if he was asked to play quarterback for a game. I don't think I would have made NFL football my career if I had to earn my money playing quarterback.

Changing the rules to protect the athletes isn't a sign of weakness or cowardice. I've gone nose-to-nose with the biggest running backs in the NFL and fought with the strongest linemen. They know for a fact that I am fearless, and no one has ever questioned my appetite for contact. But there comes a time when reason and sanity must take hold. I, for one, am not interested in answering doorbells that never rang, and the knowledge of nearly killing a wide receiver doesn't set easily on my mind. What I am trying to say is that I don't want to get injured before my scheduled retirement and I certainly don't want to send any more receivers into their early retirement. But until the rules are changed, I will continue to play the game according to the rules. My position and style of play dictate the terms with which I meet the receiver and running back. Because of the zone, it is to my advantage to sit back and wait. If I tackle at half-speed, then I only increase the chance of serious injury to myself or the probability of getting burned by some receiver. The rules can be changed to take away the high risk areas of football and still maintain that degree of hard-hitting action the fans love. As the rules now stand, there are some areas of football that bury the human side of football players and bring out the animal. For a receiver to run those patterns across the middle against the zone defense is suicide, because until the rules are changed, those assassins will be waiting in the secondary.

The rules and officiating have been a complaint of mine since my early days in the NFL, but until recently, I never gave it much thought. I always figured there was little or nothing that could be done to change the structure of NFL football. Yet now, after I have had some serious time for thinking about the problems in the structure of professional football, I see many avenues which the owners and league officials could explore. I've mentioned a few rule changes that could eliminate many of those murderous head-on tackles that break the concentration of the best receivers and strike fear into the most courageous running backs. And I have mentioned the advantages a quarterback would have with a no-blitzing rule. Obviously, these changes would give the fans more offense and offer the players a greater degree of safety. But all the rule changes in the world aren't worth a damn unless the men in the striped uniforms develop some sort of consistency with their calls. One time, I slap a running back on the head to down him and they call a fifteen yard penalty against me for unnecessary roughness. Then, during that same game, I make a tackle on a receiver and he jumps up, slugs me in the face, and wants to fight. The official just breaks up the mess. I'm talking about a game with the Steelers when I made a tackle on Lynn Swann and his emotionalism got the best of him. He missed the pass, and I guess as a reaction to this frustration, he started kicking me and jumped up and slugged me. An official was right on the spot, but instead of throwing a flag, he just pulled Swann away from me.

I have been part of the NFL since 1971 and the only consistent thing I have ever seen in the officiating was the ability to be inconsistent. Some of the officials' mistakes can be passed off as human error, and I can overlook and sympathize with those personal misjudgments. However, when individual bias is injected into the officiating, I am greatly disturbed. Swann could jump up and take a swing at me because everyone in the world knows that I could physically break him apart. Therefore, Swann is the good guy and I am the villain. So go ahead and kick the villain in the testicles, spit on him, slug him, call him dirty names, and the official will only break up the scene. But if the villain slaps a running back on the head or fights back, it becomes a situation requiring penalties and fines. To me, that is all a bunch of crap and I don't like the idea of being considered the villain. I am simply an athlete who is paid to hit. Lynn Swann is an athlete who is paid to catch passes and score touchdowns. Just because our missions during the football game are in conflict doesn't give anyone the right to label one of us a saint and the other a sinner. It all comes back to the point I'm trying to make concerning the inconsistency of the officiating. If it's wrong for me to slug anyone during the course of a game, then it's wrong for Swann or any other player in the NFL to take that type of action. The first rule in officiating must be consistency. An official should be able to act in total fairness and treat all infractions of the rules in such a manner that each type of infraction constantly carries the same penalty. When we arrive at a fair and consistent enforcement of the rules, the safety conditions and the game itself will greatly improve.

Boxing offers a good example of the type of consistent rule enforcement that is lacking in football. Professional boxing, or boxing on any level, is brutal. The purpose of a boxing match is for each opponent to make an attempt at beating the other man's head in. Yet in boxing the rules do not favor one fighter over the other. It's illegal for both fighters to hit low; neither man can butt, elbow, hit on the breaks, backhand, rabbit punch, etc. The rules apply to both contestants. In football some players, because of their position or size, can get away with infraction of the rules, while others are penalized. Professional football needs the same type of rule enforcement found in boxing.

Still, the officials, like all mortals, are subject to

errors. I strongly believe in using one judge who sits up in the press box and has the power to veto any questionable call. Since TV cameras cover everything from the antics of the fans to the cheerleaders' legs, I believe that a system could be set up that would eliminate the human factor in close calls. There are arguments from owners and league officials, who claim a camera system covering all the angles of a football game would be impossible. At the last meeting of the owners and NFL officials, they completely ruled out the use of such devices. I think they made a grave mistake. I sat at home and watched Michigan lose the Rose Bowl because of an officiating error. On a goal line play an official signaled a touchdown for Southern California, even though a Michigan defender stopped the play two yards from the end zone and caused a fumble—a fumble that Michigan recovered. The Michigan people were upset, but the official assured everyone that the back had crossed the goal line and was in the end zone before the fumble occurred. The official obviously needed to see his optometrist, because the instant replay clearly showed the back was two yards short of the goal line and he actually did fumble. Southern California ended up winning the game by exactly seven points.

In 1977 we played Denver for the American Conference Championship. The winner of the game would go on to the Super Bowl and the loser would stay home and watch it on television. During a goal line stand I got a good hit on running back Rob Lytle, and he fumbled. We recovered the ball, and our defensive team was leaving the field along with the Denver offensive team. It was a fumble, and everyone in the world who was watching the game realized it. Denver knew it was a fumble, Rob Lytle certainly knew it, I knew it, and most of the fans knew it. But somehow, and I still can't figure it out, one of the officials who must have been looking up at the blimp or something, signaled no fumble and gave the ball to Denver. They scored and won the game 21–17. Of course, after that official viewed the instant replay, he knew what the world knew when the play actually happened—it was a fumble. Like a good guy he wrote the Oakland Raiders a letter apologizing for the error. Even the Commissioner's office wrote us a nice "we're sorry" letter, too. That might have been a million-dollar mistake for the Raiders to eat, because that's just about what the team and players would have split up had we gone on to win the Super Bowl. But I couldn't very well take a letter, or, should I say, two letters of apology to my bank.

I could fill a book on bad calls made by the officials last season alone, bad calls which could have been corrected if the NFL had an official sitting in the press box watching the action. But the owners and NFL office think it would be too difficult to set up that type of equipment. Hell, I'll lend them my television, or, better yet, I'll buy them a TV, if it would help to clean up the sloppy officiating. I know that type of setup can work both ways. The Raiders have won some questionable games and lost some, but in fairness to the sport and the athletes who participate in the game, let's get a system that will improve these cloudy areas of professional football. Then "may the best team win" will be an expression with a much higher probability of coming true.

I think a replay system would also help clean up a lot of dirty action. How many times during the course of a game have you seen your favorite player get knocked out with a cheap shot the official missed? As I write, I can almost hear Pittsburgh fans screaming, "the time Atkinson hit Swann," and I'm thinking, "the time Mansfield speared me." How can a referee really be expected to call something that happens so fast only a slow-motion camera could prove it? In that type of situation, the league official could be sitting up in the press box watching several angles of replays. If he spots something cheap, he could press a little buzzer, tell the head linesman about the incident, and let the boys on the field pass judgment. That type of action would make several players around the league think before they acted. The penalty should include special fines and suspensions against the real cheap-shot artists, in addition to lost yardage at the time of the infraction.

When the camera catches someone hitting the quarterback late, or maybe a linebacker kicking a receiver in the head, the first action should be a fine. But how effective are fines? I was fined twice, and the money really didn't hurt my pocketbook one bit. Even if it is rather stiff, like the $5,000 fine Joe Greene received for his right hook to a lineman's gut, the owners of the team will sometimes sympathize with the athlete and pay the fine themselves. Then, too, even $5,000 isn't going to sting all that much when you consider some of the players' salaries. It might make you stop and think for a second, but it's still not the complete answer to the problem.

Step two in any of these criminal activities during a football game must be a severe suspension. I know that a twisted knee doesn't really start hurting until I am sitting in the stands watching my team play the game. What I'm saying is that any athlete, starting or otherwise, wants to play in the game because he loves the game. Sure, we make big money in the NFL, but for most of us professional football is a great love affair that gives us Sunday thrills. It hurts to sit out a game. More important than hurting the athlete who has committed the infraction, it also hurts the team and the team's owners. When anyone plays in the NFL, he is damn good, but there are first-string goods and second-string goods. When any member of our starting defensive unit is out with an injury, we are not totally effective. It's that way with any team. When you have starters sitting on the bench, you're in trouble. So if the league officials took this action against cheap-shot artists, the problem of dirty play would almost disappear. Every team wants to go into battle operating at 100 percent effectiveness. If players risk suspension because of serious infractions of the rules, then everyone from the athletes to the coaches, and even the owners, will handle this situation with extreme caution.

Needless to say, this type of operation must also have a high degree of consistency, and a judge must be fair. I guess what I am trying to say is there must be professionalism attached to all aspects of football if the game is to remain civilized. Otherwise, the violence and brutality is going to increase and the life expectancy of professional football players will be measured in games instead of years.

I think about Darryl Stingley and the exciting moments he'll never be able to give to the fans. I think about Gayle Sayers and how injuries ended his career before it was actually started. Even Joe Namath played as half a football player. In my estimation, Gayle Sayers was a great running back, and I enjoyed watching him play football. But he had to quit because of knee injuries, and that cheated Gayle and football fans out of years of exciting games and great runs. You simply don't replace a Gayle Sayers. Joe Namath was the most-talked-about, most-publicized quarterback in the history of the NFL. When you consider the man was crippled because of football injuries and he played every game of his career under extremely difficult conditions, he must have been one tremendous athlete. A crippled Joe Namath placed his name in the record book, but I wonder what a healthy Joe Namath would have been like.

When we watch a football game visions of touchdowns and tackles are in our mind, but the ever-present reality of football is injuries. Any athlete who has participated in a football game knows that it requires top physical condition, the best equipment, and a great deal of good luck to escape the crippling pain and punishment the years have a way of collecting within your body. And then again, for the athlete who has tasted the thrill of scoring a touchdown and making a solid tackle, there aren't any words that can describe the feeling. It's a good feeling, a great feeling, to be able to compete on a professional level and beat the best team in football or provide that game-saving play. It takes a special courage to dare to play football, but once you're hooked, it becomes a habit that can never be fully satisfied. True, I play football because I like the money, but I also love my job. When any man can arrive at that point in his life where he actually loves his work, then he is indeed a successful man. I guess it's because I love the game, and in a way I even love with a great respect the other guys that go up against me. I have one bad memory, and I don't want another. Darryl Stingley will never play football again, and maybe never walk. I can't undo yesterday's misfortune, but I might be able to prevent some of tomorrow's pain. Professional football must make that decision to change some of the rules or we are all doomed to a retirement of nursing broken bones, stiff joints, and knees that collapse. The point is to clean up football and make it safe on all levels, because with better coaching techniques and bigger and faster athletes coming into the game, people are going to start killing each other during the battle. Look into the high schools across this country of ours and see the training programs coaches have these young athletes on. Weight training, flexibility drills, diets, vitamins, and a thousand other little gimmicks and gadgets are designed to make everyone stronger, faster, and more violent. I love kids too much to see one of them share a memory similar to mine or one that might be worse. Therefore, something must be done to change the game, something that protects the safety of the athletes.

My suggested rule changes are not the answer to all the problems in football, but these changes would take the animal out of a brutal game. Football would still be a contact sport, and that part we could never change. What's more, I would never want to change the contact, because to me that is the essence of the game. But there are those areas I mentioned that could provide a great safety factor for the athletes themselves and still offer the fans the excitement of contact, scoring, and competition.

Unfortunately, they have hardly changed the rules of football, and I have this season to consider. I could play the game passively and let all the Wendell Tylers in the league run me over, but I have a deep-rooted pride that would never permit that to happen. Also, in all probability, the Raiders would never let their free safety remain passive. Either I would do the job or they would get someone else to cover my position. My job is to first of all consider the rules and regulations and then to use everything in the structure of the NFL to intimidate and discourage receivers and running backs. Since there have been few rule changes to the contrary, I can still sit back in my zone and wait for unsuspecting people to come into view. When that happens, because of what

I'm paid to do, I must be The Assassin. If and when they really change the rules, I believe that I am enough of an athlete to change my techniques. But the way everything is structured, a push-and-shove free safety may just as well play his football in a "touchy" league and not in the NFL. I care about the other athletes in the league, but I also care about me. I am not going into any more games with only half a heart.

9

AND FOR TOMORROW

A writer once wrote, "The name of one John David Tatum has not been included into the Professional Football Hall of Fame . . . yet. But his day shall come and when that event happens, the caption under his name will read, 'The Assassin.' "

When I think about my career, I hope that my achievements are not overshadowed by the title "Assassin." In reality, I am not an assassin, but rather a human being with a deep compassion for little children, young people, and my fellow athletes of the NFL. I have always resented anyone comparing me to some cheap-shot artist, because, as I have tried to explain in this book, I am only an athlete who has a job to do.

Several years ago I was visiting in Niles, Ohio, and stopped at a restaurant called Alberini's. It's a fantastic place with excellent food. I had gone there with a friend who introduced me to the manager, Ray Iezzi. Ray is a football nut and one very funny guy. He's a practical joker and the type of person who can make you laugh until your sides hurt. Ray had known me for approximately two minutes when he asked, "Jack, can I have some fun and introduce you to a guy who loves football?"

I had no objections, so Ray called one of his bartenders over and asked, "Art, the three of us have been having a terrible argument and I want you to settle the issue once and for all. Tell us who you think the meanest, dirtiest, hardest-hitting, rottenest bastard who ever played the game of football. Think about it, Art; a no-good bastard who hits like a ton of bricks."

Obviously, Art didn't know who I was. He stood there for only a second thinking about his answer and then blurted out, "Hell, that's got to be Jack Tatum of the Oakland Raiders. I saw him nearly kill Lynn Swann down in Pittsburgh."

"Art," Ray said with a peculiar grin on his face, "meet Jack Tatum."

Art's lower jaw dropped to the floor and with an embarrassed look, he tried to explain, "I don't mean you're a dirty player, you just hit."

I knew what the man meant, and the incident was funny. Art was a man who knew football and football players. He honestly didn't mean I was a cheap-shot artist; it's just that I do hit. Maybe now, after reading my book, more fans will understand that I am only a human being and not some villainous character you want to hate. I realize that getting my name in the record book as only an athlete and not as an assassin will, in all probability, be an uphill battle. But my real battle is out there in the world, and that's the fight I want to win. I'm talking, of course, about the young people; the people who live in a ghetto or spend their days looking out into the world from a hospital bed; the people who have lost hope and faith; the people for whom yesterday is a bitter memory and tomorrow offers only more pain and suffering. I know that I'll never be able to change the course this world is traveling, but I will be able to do my small part.

Every year I go back to Passaic for business and just to visit old friends and make new ones. I have a scholarship fund going in Passaic, and each year they have a banquet. It's a good cause, and I know that because of my name and a little effort some kid in the ghetto is going to get a chance at college and the opportunity to move out into the world. Still, there are more reasons for my trip to Passaic than just my scholarship fund. I always go back into the ghetto and talk with the young people there. I tell them about being tough and what it takes to become a man. Sometimes the kids listen, while other times they don't. I explain to them that being tough isn't buying or selling drugs, nor is it taking part in knife fights or robberies or murders. Tough is rising above all the adversity and going out into the world and actually making everything work. Anybody who feels sorry for himself because he was born and raised in a ghetto is going to die in the ghetto. To me, the ghetto was a blessing, because now I can appreciate my life and can share everything I have learned throughout the years. No one can tell me that I don't understand their side of life, because I was there and I lived it. But more important, I had a plan, a dream, and I worked it to the best of my ability. Now I play football in the NFL and my financial security is assured. Maybe I was lucky, but then again, maybe a man earns his own luck in this world.

I feel for the kids in the ghetto, but they do have young bodies and minds that can, if they are properly used, overcome adversity. The little kids who live in hospital beds and are deprived of good health are the ones my heart goes out to more than anyone else. I find it rewarding to spend time visiting these youngsters in the hospital, and I try to give them hope. That's all I can really do for those little people, but the young man in the ghetto can get up and walk into a better life on his own—if he has the fortitude.

I know it is tough for those kids from underprivileged homes to have hope, but when I sit on the edge of some little kid's hospital bed and see his skinny legs and braces, it makes me want to cry. I know this little man will never have the chance to run and play or even stand up and walk, and then I think about what tough really is. I had the courage to dare to be different while growing up in the ghetto, and I have the toughness to play professional football, but at the same time I realize how much more strong-willed some of those little children in hospitals across our land must be just to accept a yesterday, today, and tomorrow of the same painful memories and same limited hope. My life is a fantastic adventure. I have the ability to move about and see the world, but there are some who are handicapped by physical and mental restriction, and for them, my heart cries. I really care about people and what happens to this world, but from my exposure in professional football, I have been dubbed an assassin without morals and ethics. Well, surprise, football players are human, too.

If anyone spent a day with me, they might be astonished. At heart, I'm just a homebody, or more accurately, I'm still that little country boy who loved to sit and listen to his grandfather's stories. I don't go in for wild parties, heavy drinking, or running with fifty or sixty different ladies. I enjoy privacy, a quiet life, and the company of just a few good lady friends. I know the stability of some of my football buddies might be questionable, but the fans should understand that football is one thing, while life is quite another. Skip Thomas, Clarence Davis, and George Atkinson might be characters on the field of battle, but most of the time they are quite different in real life. Clarence, George, and I enjoy chess and a quiet game of pool. I'm not talking about barroom pool. George and Clarence have pool tables at their homes and we have some serious games. Even Skip is different in real life, most of the time, at least.

Several years ago we played in San Diego, and the night before the game Skip was having problems. He had refused to talk with reporters, told the front desk "no calls," and just wanted to be off alone with himself. Then a friend of mine stopped by our room with his little boy. Skip was under the covers and had four or five pillows over his face. He didn't want to be disturbed until he heard the little kid's voice. That was it, and before I knew what happened Skip was up and talking to the little dude about professional football, life, Corvettes, and motorcycles.

Football is a strange game and does strange things to the athletes. There are mental pressures, physical pressures, and the overall uncertainties of your future. One day I could be the most aggressive tackler in the NFL and the next day I could be lying flat on my back in a hospital bed with a broken neck.

Darryl Stingley will probably never walk again and that really tears at me. I don't like to pass off the incident as "just part of the game," because it sounds calloused and hard, but during contact, serious injuries can and often do occur. I realize it is impossible to undo what happened to Darryl, but at the same time I can think about his tomorrow. Right now, I'd like to start a special fund-raising program to help with his medical bills and give his family the things he worked for during his time in the NFL. Football is a brutal game, but there is still room for sentiment. Like I said, I care.

In planning for my tomorrow, I know that my NFL days are numbered, and when my time is over I must be able to accept the fact and move into something else. Physically, I feel good, but now it requires a lot more work to get the body into shape, and it takes a little longer to shake the bumps of a game. Maybe two more years, or possibly three, I don't really know, but it's just a matter of time before I have to retire. Hopefully, I won't be like the fighter who goes one round too many. Hopefully, I'll have the intelligence to recognize the signs and be able to walk away from my NFL career. I believe that I will have the wisdom to do the right thing, because that's the way my life has always been slanted.

When I hang up the cleats, I think I'll become a farmer or rancher. I like the outdoors and have my eyes on some land in Southern California. Right now that's my dream, but my reality is the still the NFL. Another season is upon me and the press has started writing about the villainous character wearing the silver and black. Maybe because of my style of play I am The Assassin, but at heart I'm a friendly assassin who honestly cares about people and the world.